Truth & spirituality
contemporary issues

GCSE RELIGIOUS STUDIES FOR AQA B

Michael Keene

Acknowledgements

The author and publisher would like to thank the following for the use of copyright material:

ACE photo agency/Steve Cavalier on p. 31; Alex Keene/The Walking Camera on pp. 3, 4, 5, 8, 9, 11, 12, 13, 15, 17, 19, 23, 24, 27, 35, 45, 47, 53, 59, 61, 62, 69, 71, 81, 83, 87, 93, 102, 103, 107, 114, 115, 119, 121 (x2), 129, 133, 135; BBC Picture Archives on p. 95; Christine Osborne Pictures on pp. 25, 117, 131; Collection Hyphen Films on pp. 85, 98; Corbis on pp. 109, 127; David Hoffman Photo Library on p. 116; Digital Stock on pp. 1, 16, 20, 49, 60, 99; EMPICS on p. 73; Getty Images/ The Image Bank/GDT on p. 89; Help the Aged on p. 126; John Birdsall Social Issues Photolibrary on pp. 37, 43; Mirrorpix.com on p. 75; Network Photographers on p. 113; PA Photos on p. 104, 105; Rex on pp. 18, 41, 50, 55, 96, Rex/Remo Casilli on p. 21, Rex/J Sutton Hibbert on p. 39, Rex/Rob Judges on p. 51, Rex/Patsy Lynch on p. 57, Rex/Tamara Beckwith on p. 63, Rex/Simon Roberts on p. 70, Rex/Patrick Barth on p. 77, Rex/Tim Rooke on p. 91, Rex/Brendan Beirne on p. 112; Reuters/Yves Herman on p. 111, Reuters/George Mulala on p. 123; Robert Harding on p. 101, Robert Harding/Tettoni Casio on p. 7, Robert Harding/JHC Wilson on p. 65; Science Photo Library/Pascal Goetgheluck on p. 67; Still Pictures/Bojan Brecelj on p. 14, Still Pictures/Ingrid Moorjohn on p. 29, Still Pictures/Shehzad Noorani on pp. 33, 125

Cover images: Joanne O'Brien/Format, Lisa Woollett/Format, Digital Stock

© 2002 Folens Limited, on behalf of the author.

United Kingdom: Folens Publishers, Apex Business Centre, Boscombe Road, Dunstable, LU5 4RL.
Email: folens@folens.com

Ireland: Folens Publishers, Greenhills Road, Tallaght, Dublin 24.
Email: info@folens.ie

Poland: JUKA, ul. Renesansowa 38, Warsaw 01-905.

Folens allows photocopying of pages marked 'copiable page' for educational use, providing that this use is within the confines of the purchasing institution. Copiable pages should not be declared in any return in respect of any photocopying licence.

Folens publications are protected by international copyright laws. All rights are reserved. The copyright of all materials in this publication, except where otherwise stated, remains the property of the publisher and author. No part of this publication may be reproduced, stored in a retrieval system, or transmitted, in any form or by any means, for whatever purpose, without the written permission of Folens Limited.

Michael Keene hereby asserts his moral right to be identified as the author of this work in accordance with the Copyright, Designs and Patents Act 1988.

Editor: Melody Ismail

Design: FMS Design Consultants Limited.

First published 2002 by Folens Limited.
Reprinted 2003.

Every effort has been made to trace the copyright holders of material used in this publication. If any copyright holder has been overlooked, we should be pleased to make any necessary arrangements.

British Library Cataloguing in Publication Data. A catalogue record for this publication is available from the British Library.

ISBN 1 84303 294 5

Truth, spirituality and contemporary issues

Contents

Introduction — v

CHAPTER 1: Truth and spirituality — 1

1:1	Different kinds of truth	2
1:2	The spiritual dimension	4
1:3	Searching for the truth	6
1:4	The holy books	8
1:5	Religious authorities	10
1:6	Faith communities and voluntary organisations	12
1:7	Religious worship	14
1:8	Religious symbols	16
1:9	Religious piety	18
1:10	The creative spirit	20
1:11	Truth and spirituality in Christianity	22
1:12	Truth and spirituality in Judaism and Islam	24
1:13	Truth and spirituality in Hinduism, Sikhism and Buddhism	26
Exam help …		28

CHAPTER 2: Matters of life — 29

2:1	The beginning of life	30
2:2	The sanctity of life	32
2:3	Fertility and infertility	34
2:4	Genetic engineering	36
2:5	Cloning	38
2:6	Organ transplants and blood transfusions	40
2:7	Christianity and matters of life	42
2:8	Judaism and Islam, and matters of life	44
2:9	Hinduism, Sikhism and Buddhism, and matters of life	46
Exam help …		48

CHAPTER 3: Matters of death — 49

3:1	The sick and the elderly	50
3:2	The hospice movement	52
3:3	Euthanasia – the facts	54
3:4	Voluntary euthanasia – the issues	56
3:5	Suicide	58
3:6	Christianity and matters of death	60
3:7	Judaism and Islam, and matters of death	62
3:8	Hinduism, Sikhism and Buddhism, and matters of death	64
Exam help …		66

CHAPTER 4: Drug abuse — 67

4:1	Drugs	68
4:2	Legal drugs	70
4:3	Drugs in sport	72
4:4	Class A drugs	74
4:5	Class B drugs	76
4:6	Christianity and drugs	78
4:7	Judaism and Islam, and drugs	80
4:8	Hinduism, Sikhism and Buddhism, and drugs	82

Exam help … 84

CHAPTER 5: Media and technology — 85

5:1	What are the media?	86
5:2	The effects of the media	88
5:3	Controlling the media	90
5:4	Religious broadcasting	92
5:5	Christianity and the media	94
5:6	Judaism and Islam, and the media	96
5:7	Hinduism, Sikhism and Buddhism, and the media	98

Exam help … 100

CHAPTER 6: Crime and punishment — 101

6:1	Crime	102
6:2	Punishment	104
6:3	Ways of punishing	106
6:4	Capital punishment – the facts	108
6:5	Capital punishment – the issues	110
6:6	Christianity and punishment	112
6:7	Judaism and Islam, and punishment	114
6:8	Hinduism, Sikhism and Buddhism, and punishment	116

Exam help …

CHAPTER 7: Rich and poor — 119

7:1	The rich	120
7:2	The poor (1)	122
7:3	The poor (2)	124
7:4	Looking after the poor	126
7:5	The Lotto	128
7:6	Christianity and wealth	130
7:7	Judaism and Islam, and wealth	132
7:8	Hinduism, Sikhism and Buddhism, and wealth	134

Exam help … 136

Glossary — 137

Useful contacts — 143

Index — 145

Truth, spirituality and contemporary issues

Introduction

You have chosen to study specification B of the AQA examination in Religious Studies. This textbook has been prepared to give you the best possible chance of doing well in this examination. Whilst planning this textbook we have taken great care to make it suitable for those taking both the long and short course options. We hope that you will find it both an interesting introduction to some very important topics and a book that is easy-to-use.

As you use this book you will notice, in particular, the following key features.

- The material is presented in the same order, and uses the same language, as the AQA syllabus itself. This is a real advantage. It means that if you carefully work your way through this book you will cover everything that the exam board requires of you. To help you further the material is presented in easy-to-digest, bite-sized chunks that are broken down by frequent sub-headings.

- An introduction leads you into each topic gradually. It then goes on to outline the main issues and questions that you are going to be looking at.

- A 'key question' at the beginning of the text introduces you to the most important issue in each spread. This is a good place to start. It helps you to focus your mind as you read what follows. It also cuts straight to the chase and lets you know what really matters.

- You will find significant words or phrases, when they are first introduced, listed under 'Important words'. You should try to learn as many of these as you can. Try to use them appropriately in your exam answers to give real depth.

IMPORTANT WORDS

Guru Granth Sahib; the holy book of the Sikh religion
Qur'an; the sacred book of Islam, revealed by Allah to the Prophet Muhammad
Ten Commandments; part of the 613 commandments in the Torah
Torah; 'law', the first five books of the Jewish Scriptures

- Other words that you will come across in the text are explained in the 'Glossary' at the end of the book. When you come across a word that you have not met before be sure to look it up in the glossary. It will only take you a minute and will help you understand the text more easily. It is a good idea to keep your own dictionary of technical words that you can add to as you go along.

- You will find the teachings of the different religions on the various topics colour-coded to help you to find your way around.

v

Truth, spirituality and contemporary issues

Introduction continued ...

- There are many quotations taken from the holy books, and other sources, dotted throughout the book. These are very important. They matter to the followers of the different religions but they also help you to understand why people believe what they do. Learn as many of them as you can. Try to use them in your examination answers.
- Throughout the book you will find various 'Exam tips'. Put the advice that you are given into practice and you will find your work improve noticeably. There is a skill involved in taking exams and these tips will help improve your exam techniques.

> ✓ **Exam tip**
> In the case of euthanasia and other social topics, candidates must know both sides of the argument. You should look in the newspapers for current examples. New and different circumstances are always arising. Use relevant and up-to-date information in your answers.

- Many spreads include a 'Think about' exercise. These encourage you to think about something that you have read. It is very easy to move through a course quickly without taking time out to think about some of the things that you have learned. Remember – in this course you are expected to learn about religion and also to learn from it. The 'Think about' questions are there to help you to apply the teachings of the world religions to very specific social, moral and personal issues. To do this you must regularly stop and think.

> **Think about ...**
> Look at the survey findings above. For which conditions did more than 50 per cent of those interviewed think that voluntary euthanasia should be allowed? Write down **TWO** comments to show how you feel about these findings.
> Do you think that they give a true indication of how the majority of people feel about euthanasia? Give **TWO** reasons for your answer.

- The 'Tasks' have been carefully chosen to help you to concentrate on the most important areas that you have studied. If you pay them attention they will direct you to those areas that you need to concentrate on.

> **Tasks**
> 1. Give ONE example of:
>   a. a scientific truth b. a historical truth
>   c. a moral truth   d. a spiritual truth.
> 2. Where do people look when they are searching for religious truth?

- There is a 'Summary' at the end of each spread. This gives you the key points of that spread. These summaries will help you to remember what you have learned before you move on to the next issue. When the exam draws near they can also be used as part of your revision programme.

SUMMARY

1 Most religious people search for the truth in the teachings, holy books and worship experiences of their faith.

2 There are different kinds of truth – scientific, historical, moral and spiritual. Faith plays an important part in reaching moral and spiritual truth.

- There are also carefully selected photographs that go with each spread. These are large enough for you to be able to learn a great deal from the detail. Do not rush past them without stopping to look and learn.
- Finally, each section in the book ends with worked GCSE questions. This 'Exam help' is included to show you what should be contained within a full exam answer. They are in note form and are intended to point you in the right direction. Use them to stimulate your own answers to the questions.

So, enough of the introduction. Time to get started. Enjoy!

CHAPTER 1
Truth and spirituality

In this opening chapter we will be looking at the nature of truth and spirituality. Some of the areas we will be covering are quite complicated and abstract. You will be provided with concrete examples so that you can see the meaning and relevance of the material for those people who belong to the different religions. We will be looking at two questions throughout the chapter:

What is truth?

Our basic question here will be: What do we mean when we say that something is true? You will soon discover that the question has more than one answer – depending on who is asked. For example, a scientist will provide you with one answer, a historian another, a musician a third and a religious believer a fourth. They are all giving you legitimate answers to the question. They are simply answering the question from different points of view. No one has a monopoly on truth. As far as religious truth is concerned, a mixture of reason, belief, experience, trust and faith are all involved.

What is spirituality?

Spirituality is a much wider idea than most people realise. It includes such traditional activities as reading the holy books, prayer and meditation, taking part in acts of worship and visiting holy places. It also includes, for some people, belonging to a 'faith community' although this will not necessarily be the case for everyone. For many, spirituality includes a 'sense of God's presence', which can be gained from listening to a piece of music, being in a beautiful place or looking at a majestic work of art. These experiences provide people with the opportunity to 'look inwardly and speak outwardly'. Often your own life and experiences will provide you with the necessary starting points from which you can begin to express, and understand, what the word 'spirituality' means.

TRUTH AND SPIRITUALITY

1:1 Different kinds of truth

What is truth?

It was Pontius Pilate, the Roman governor of Judaea, who during the trial of Jesus asked the question – 'What is the truth?' This is a difficult question to answer, partly because *truth* itself is so difficult to understand. For our purposes, there are three kinds of truth.

1. **Scientific truth.** We base most of our life on the assumption that there are many things about the world in which we live that we can assume to be true. We accept them as true because we can observe them to be so. Take just one example: it takes the earth a year to move around the sun. The earth is slightly tilted so, during the year, parts of the earth are closer to the sun than other parts – this produces the different seasons. All the available evidence plus our own limited observations lead us to believe that this scientific hypothesis (theory) is true. It is unlikely that our understanding of this will change but, in the nature of scientific truth, startling new evidence could come to light at any time, which might force us to change this conclusion.

   Scientific truth is based on what we know, and the conclusions we draw, at the time. Science proceeds through experiment and repeated testing. It must be possible for an experiment to be conducted and the same conclusion reached each time before scientific truth can be established. We must be prepared to change our understanding if the evidence compels us to do so.

2. **Historical truth.** Once events have occurred they cannot be changed. All that can change is the way in which we understand them. However, factual explanations are open to different interpretations: how people interpret an event can have a direct link to how historical events can be understood. There is plenty of documentary evidence to confirm that the Normans invaded Britain in 1066 and that King John signed the Magna Carta in 1215 at Runnymede. These historical 'facts' are unchallenged. Our understanding of their significance in the later history of the UK continues to grow almost a thousand years after the events.

   Comparatively new sciences, such as archaeology, are also constantly bringing us new knowledge about the past. We are still not sure, for instance, the exact age of Stonehenge, but new discoveries in 2002 held out fresh hope that this historical puzzle might soon be solved. Our knowledge of historical truth is growing all the time.

3. **Spiritual and moral truth.** Spiritual and moral truths are very different from scientific and historical truths. Religious people believe that the truth can be found in three places.

- In the life, example and teachings of an outstanding religious teacher such as Jesus (Christianity), Muhammad (Islam) or the Buddha (Buddhism). These figures provide inspiration for millions of people in the modern world. Amongst the religions covered in this book only Hinduism does not depend on such a figure.

- In the teachings of a holy book or books. Jews look to the Torah; Christians to the Bible; Muslims to the Qur'an and Sikhs to the Guru Granth Sahib for the truth. Hindus and Buddhists have many such holy books.

- In belonging to a faith community. Communal acts of prayer and worship are an important part of the search for religious truth for many people. Religious faith and understanding form a journey that most people share with others. This is why worship is at the heart of religious experience. There are moral 'truths' on which we base our lives. Some people take their moral beliefs from their religious faith. A Jew, for example, believes that adultery is wrong because the Ten Commandments forbid it. A non-religious person may also believe that adultery is wrong. Religious and non-religious people may follow similar moral codes and live their lives by similar standards – but for very different reasons.

> *Jesus answered Pilate: "I was born and came into the world for this one purpose, to speak about the truth. Whoever belongs to the truth listens to me."*
>
> *"And what is truth?" Pilate asked.*
>
> ... **THE BIBLE (JOHN 18.37–38)**

Reason can take us much of the way towards reaching the truth in important areas of life, such as science and the past, but it has its limitations. It can only be based on what we know now, yet our knowledge is growing all the time. Sometimes equally qualified people working with the same body of information will reach different conclusions! Reason as well as faith and belief can help people in the search for religious truth.

▲ The Guru Granth Sahib is the most important source of truth for all Sikhs. It symbolises God's presence with them.

✓ Exam tip
There are many important words in this book with which you might not be familiar. It is important that you learn the meaning of these words. If you do this it will give your exam answers real depth. There are 'important words' boxes throughout, with fuller explanations in the glossary.

Tasks
1. Give **ONE** example of:
   a. a scientific truth b. a historical truth
   c. a moral truth   d. a spiritual truth.
2. Where do people look when they are searching for religious truth?

IMPORTANT WORDS

Guru Granth Sahib; the holy book of the Sikh religion
Qur'an; the sacred book of Islam, revealed by Allah to the Prophet Muhammad
Ten Commandments; part of the 613 commandments in the Torah
Torah; 'law', the first five books of the Jewish Scriptures

SUMMARY

❶ Most religious people search for the truth in the teachings, holy books and worship experiences of their faith.

❷ There are different kinds of truth – scientific, historical, moral and spiritual. Faith plays an important part in reaching moral and spiritual truth.

3

TRUTH AND SPIRITUALITY

1:2 The spiritual dimension

What are the main differences between a materialistic and a spiritual approach to life?

There are two dimensions to life – the material and the spiritual. Many people in the modern world, however, fail even to recognise that the spiritual dimension exists. The Bhagavad Gita, an ancient Hindu holy book, warned of this danger centuries ago.

The material dimension

It is often said that we now live in a 'consumer society'. We buy and use goods of all kinds – clothes, food, electrical goods, cars and so on. Advertisers pressure us to buy, use and discard more and more of them. The mobile phone, for example, is an excellent example of this. It was a luxury in 1997, a fashion accessory in 1999 and a necessity in 2002. Now that the UK market is saturated and most people have a mobile phone, new ways of marketing and selling the product must be found.

Spending priorities have changed. People who were once concerned to acquire the basic necessities of life, now want to eat out more or buy a DVD player. Many people are always aiming to update their computer or phone to take advantage of the latest technology. What people cannot afford they may choose to pay for with credit cards: it has been said that we are now living in a 'plastic culture'. It often seems as if people are increasingly convinced that the secret of happiness and success is possessing as many material goods as possible – they are 'materialists'.

The spiritual dimension

> *What good will it be for a man if he gains the whole world yet forfeits his soul? Or what can a man give in exchange for his soul?*
>
> **... THE BIBLE (MATTHEW 16.26)**

▼ In the consumer society many people find their deepest satisfaction in buying goods, often using a loan or credit to do so.

The materialist is said not to recognise that human beings have a spirit or soul, with spiritual needs that must be met. Yet 'the spiritual dimension' is a very important part of everyone's life. It may show itself in a variety of ways.

1. In the search for the meaning of life – a search in which everyone is involved in some way or other.
2. In an awareness of that which lies beyond material life when feelings of awe, wonder or mystery are experienced. These experiences may come when listening to a piece of music, looking at a painting, reading a poem, surveying a breathtaking view or standing in a beautiful building.
3. Exploring the inner world of inspiration and creativity. Art, creative writing and composing music are ways of doing this.
4. An awareness of self-identity and self-worth. A person may find this through the paid work they do or voluntary work in which they are involved.
5. A recognition of the values of the world and other people. Love between two people or experiencing the feeling of a special moment may be the closest that most people come to having a spiritual experience.
6. Closeness to the Divine: for some people it may be one of the experiences above that brings this about. For others it may be taking part in a religious experience in a place of worship.

All of these experiences point to the existence of a spiritual dimension. They are experiences known, in some shape or other, to almost everyone. Many people act like materialists at times but, deep down, they often acknowledge that there is more to life than money and possessions – as Jesus pointed out *(see quotation)*.

Tasks

1. a. What do we mean when we speak of living in a 'consumer society'?
   b. What do we mean by 'materialism'?
   c. Write down **TWO** characteristics of a materialistic attitude to life.
2. a. What is the spiritual dimension?
   b. Write down **FIVE** different experiences that might lead many people to conclude that there is a spiritual dimension to life.
   c. Would you describe these experiences as spiritual experiences? Give **ONE** reason for your answer.
3. Listen to a special piece of music, watch a video showing the beauty of the natural world or visit a beautiful place of worship and either produce a piece of creative writing or paint a picture to show what feelings the experience evoked within you.

IMPORTANT WORDS

Materialism; an approach to life based on the assumption that material possessions are more important than spiritual values

Spirituality; an approach to life based on the assumption that there are important spiritual values

 Think about ...

Do you think that the majority of people today are materialists or do most people believe that there is a spiritual dimension to life? How do you think a spiritual dimension shows itself in most people?

SUMMARY

1 Some people have a materialistic attitude to life, which is based on the accumulation of material goods. The spiritual element does not seem to play any part in their search for happiness.

2 Many people have a spiritual dimension that recognises the importance of spiritual values. These people may not belong to an organised religion. They may not even recognise that their life has a spiritual dimension.

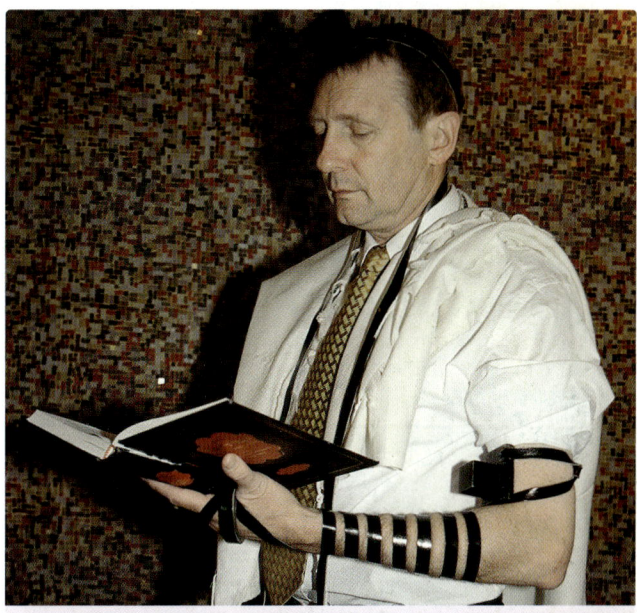

▲ When a Jewish man wears his tefillin to pray he is showing that he recognises the importance of the spiritual dimension in his life.

TRUTH AND SPIRITUALITY

1:3 Searching for the truth

What is the link between faith and truth?

Religious belief demands faith since it cannot be proved as if it were scientific truth. For Jews and Christians this is faith in Almighty God; for Muslims it is faith in the all-powerful Allah; for Hindus it is faith in Brahman, the Supreme Spirit; and for Sikhs it is faith in Nam. Of all the religious believers in this book, Buddhists do not believe in God. Most religious people have faith in a God who gives meaning to their lives. They follow the religion that helps them to make best sense of that faith.

Faith and the truth

Religions do not all say the same thing. They have different stories to tell because their histories are very different. They draw on the life-stories and teachings of very different people. They have different beliefs. They offer different ways of life to their followers. They express themselves in different ways through their worship. Each religion is offering a version of the truth and each demands faith from its followers. Faith is very important in religion. Faith brings a worshipper into spiritual contact and fellowship with God. It is impossible to be a Christian or a Sikh, for example, without having faith.

The Qur'an says that it is the men and woman who have faith in God who are rich; not those who have money in the bank. The Qur'an explains that Muslims who have faith in God will show it in their everyday lives by turning away from idle talk and gossip, as well as being active in almsgiving (giving money to the poor).

Most religious people do not believe that their religion is a part of the truth but that it *is* the truth. This explains why a Christian is a Christian and not a Muslim, or why a Sikh belongs to that religion and not Hinduism. Each person is drawn to the faith that seems to take them closest to the truth. This truth is believed to be found in the holy books and in the religious founders and leaders who inspire faith and trust in their followers. Followers of each religion must accept the teaching of the holy books and the religious authorities. They are not free to accept parts of the faith and reject others – although people often do!

The conscience

In order to know how to behave, most religious people follow the teaching of the holy books they respect and look to various religious leaders for inspiration and guidance. They also look within themselves, to their own conscience, as an important source of truth. The Book of Common Prayer, the old Anglican prayer book, says that we should all stand in awe (great fear) before our conscience, since it is the voice of God in our inmost being *(see quotation)*. This is a conclusion with which followers of most religions would agree.

> *Stand in awe, and sin not; commune with your own heart, and in your chamber, and be still.*
>
> **... THE BOOK OF COMMON PRAYER**

To religious people the conscience may be the voice of God, but it is much more than that. It reflects our upbringing and the moral standards that were taught to us. The standards of our parents, our school and the society in which we live all play a part in determining what our conscience tells us. Above all else, it reflects what we know in our inmost being to be right and truthful. For example, most people agree that murder is wrong but, even then, it is up to us whether or not we do what our conscience tells us.

Our conscience can inform us about the right course of action but it cannot compel us to do the right thing. That is down to our free will. Although some religions question whether we are really free, it is difficult to see how we can be held accountable by God for our actions unless we are. In many situations it is not easy to know exactly what our conscience is telling us. Many of the situations in which we find ourselves are not clear-cut. Sometimes what we take to be the voice of God is obscured by circumstances.

> ✓ **Exam tip**
> There are some subjects, like the conscience, which are abstract and difficult to explain. When answering such a question try to root your answer in real life by giving everyday examples.

IMPORTANT WORDS

Allah;	the name of the Supreme Being worshipped by Muslims
Brahman;	the holy power believed by Hindus to be behind the universe
Nam;	word used in Sikhism for God

▲ Young Buddhists worshipping together. Worship is an important aspect of seeking religious truth.

Tasks

1. Explain what religious people mean when they say that they have faith in God.
2. a. What do you think your 'conscience' is?
   b. How do you know that you have a conscience?
   c. Where do you think your conscience comes from?
   d. Do you think that your conscience is a good guide to follow or not? Give **TWO** reasons for your answer.
3. Write **ONE** paragraph about:
   a. Allah b. Brahman
   c. Nam

SUMMARY

1 Religious people look to their religion to provide them with the truth. This truth is believed to lie mainly with the religious leaders and in the holy books that they respect.

2 People, religious and non-religious, also look to their conscience to guide them in their moral decision-making. For religious people this may be the 'voice of God' but to the person who does not believe in God, it may be little more than the sum of their social experience.

3 Everyone has the free will to reject what their conscience tells them. Most religions teach that they will finally be held to account for their actions.

TRUTH AND SPIRITUALITY

1:4 The holy books

Why are the holy books important to religious people?

Each religion has its own holy books or scriptures. In some cases there is just one holy book, such as the Bible in Christianity, the Qur'an in Islam and the Guru Granth Sahib in Sikhism. Other religions, such as Hinduism and Buddhism, each have many holy books.

The importance of the holy books

The holy books carry great authority for the followers of the different religions and reading from them is an important part of public and private worship. In many church services, for example, there are three readings from the Bible – from the Old Testament, from the Gospels and from the letters in the New Testament, especially those written by St Paul. Sikhs sit below a copy of the Guru Granth Sahib in the gurdwara to show their respect because it symbolises the presence of God with them in their worship. On important family and communal occasions in the Sikh community there is a non-stop 48-hour reading of the holy book, called an 'Akhand Path', as Sikhs try to understand what God is saying to them. A random opening of the Guru Granth Sahib determines the first letter of the first name of a new Sikh baby.

> We hold that the Qur'an is the uncreated speech of God, and that he who holds the creation [human writing] of the Qur'an is an unbeliever.
>
> **... TENTH-CENTURY MUSLIM, WRITING ABOUT THE QUR'AN**

▼ An open Bible in a church. Christians attach great importance to their holy book.

Inspiration

By any standards the holy books are remarkable. Some of the Hindu holy books (Vedas), for example, are amongst the oldest known books. The oldest parts of the Jewish Scriptures date from about 4000 BCE. All of the books of the Christian Bible were written by around the end of the first century CE and collected together into one book by the fourth century CE. Age alone, however, would not guarantee the authority of the holy books for religious believers.

The holy books carry great authority because they are believed to have come from God. The Qur'an is the classic example. This holy book contains the revelations that Muslims believe Allah gave to the Prophet Muhammad. The Prophet passed them on to his followers just as he had received them from God. Later the followers wrote them down just as they had received them, so setting up an unbroken link between God and the book. This encourages Muslims to look on the Qur'an as the actual 'word of God' and it is this that gives the Qur'an its authority.

There are many Christians who believe the same thing about the Bible. They take their cue from St Paul *(see quotation)* although his words about the scriptures only applied to the Old Testament. These Christians, called 'fundamentalists', believe that the Bible is free of any error from start to finish. Other Christians believe that the writers of the books in the Bible were 'inspired' by God in some way, therefore this does not mean that the Bible is free from error. It may include some factual errors but nothing can detract from its spiritual power and authority for Christian believers.

> All Scripture is inspired by God and is useful for teaching the truth, rebuking error, correcting faults, and giving instruction for right living ...
>
> **... THE BIBLE (2 TIMOTHY 3.16)**

Clearly the holy books need to be studied and understood. Readers need to know that each holy book contains many different kinds of writing. A straightforward piece of history, for instance, needs to be approached differently to a parable or a piece of poetry. Even then believers may disagree over the way they understand the teachings of the holy books. An example of this is the teaching of the Qur'an on jihad (holy war). Jihad is meant to be a spiritual struggle against sin.

As the events of 11 September 2001 in America show, a minority of Muslim 'extremists' use the teaching to argue jihad requires a military action.

In the end, though, religious people read their holy books because they believe that they hear the voice of God speaking to them through the pages. Holy books are a great source of truth, capable of nourishing the spiritual faith of believers.

IT'S A FACT

The much-loved Hindu poem, the *Mahabharata*, has over 100 000 verses and is the longest known poem. It is also one of the oldest known books dating back to around 400BCE. The poem was filmed in 1989 and shown on television. The film is 6 hours long.

Tasks

1. Write down the names of **THREE** holy books and the religions to which they belong.
2. Both Christians and Muslims use the phrase 'the word of God' to describe their holy books. What do you think they mean when they use this phrase in their worship?
3. Give **TWO** examples, taken from different religions, which show how much importance is attached to the holy books.
4. Religious people treat their holy books with great respect. Find out **TWO** ways in which this great respect for the holy book shows itself. You can draw your two examples from Christianity, Judaism, Islam or Sikhism.

IMPORTANT WORDS

Gospels;	the four books in the New Testament that record the life and teachings of Jesus
New Testament;	the second part of the Christian bible
Old Testament;	the first part of the Christian bible, corresponding approximately to the Jewish Scriptures
St Paul;	prominent leader in the early Christian church

SUMMARY

1. Each religion has its own holy books or scriptures. These are treated with the greatest respect – especially in Islam and Sikhism. Reading from them is a very important part of private and public worship.

2. The holy books are very old and this gives them part of their authority. Their main authority, however, comes from their divine origins – they are believed to be 'the word of God'. Muslims and many Christians believe this to be true about the Qur'an and the Bible.

3. To understand the holy books they must be read and studied. They contain many different kinds of writings which must be understood. Religious people read them to hear God speaking to them today.

▼ As a sign of respect to the Qur'an, Muslims do not place the holy book on the ground.

TRUTH AND SPIRITUALITY

1:5 Religious authorities

Who are the religious authorities and what part do they play in the lives of most religious believers?

Clearly the holy books, and their teachings, play a very important part in the lives of most religious believers. Special times are set apart in most religions when the holy books can be studied. Jewish men, for instance, spend some part of every Sabbath day in pairs studying the Torah. Studying the Bible is important for most Christians and this is done daily and especially, in many churches, in the weeks leading up to the festival of Easter. Muslims set aside special time to study the Qur'an during the festival of Ramadan.

The importance of tradition

Most religions attach great importance to any traditions that go back to the earliest years of the faith. These traditions are very important because they have stood the test of time. Christianity and Judaism provide good examples of this.

- Both the Roman Catholic Church and the Orthodox Church trace their origins back to the earliest years of the Christian faith. For their most important service, the Holy Liturgy, Orthodox Christians use a form of words that goes back to the fourth century CE.
- In the Jewish faith, the tradition of the Exodus is celebrated each year in the festival of Passover and is considered by Jews to be the greatest event in their history. After leaving Egyptian slavery, by God's intervention over 2000 years ago, the Jews spent 40 years travelling to their Promised Land of Canaan (now called Israel). This intervention by God on their behalf in the past gives Jews their confidence in God today. Jews still believe in a God who is able to perform miracles.

> **Exam tip**
> It is important to be able to link religious practices today with their origins in the past. You should know, for instance, about the historical events that are celebrated during the festivals of Passover, Christmas and Easter.

Religious leaders

> *The Guru [religious teacher] is the ladder, the dinghy, the raft by means of which one reaches God; the Guru is the lake, the ocean, the boat, the sacred place of pilgrimage, the river. Without the Guru there can be no love.*
>
> **... THE HYMNS OF GURU NANAK**

Religious leaders are important, for various reasons, whether they are rabbis, imams, priests or gurus.

- They help to maintain the religious traditions of the faith. They are the custodians of the past and are expected to hand the religious traditions they have inherited down to the next generation.
- They help people to understand their faith. The main task of rabbis and imams is essentially a teaching one.
- They lead people in their acts of worship. This is particularly true in a religion such as Christianity, where the priest is often seen as an intermediary, a go-between, bringing together God and the worshippers.
- They explain the meaning of the holy books. This usually happens within the context of prayer. An important part of prayer in the mosque every Friday is the sermon in which a part of the Qur'an is explained.
- They attract new converts to the faith. Christianity, for example, is a missionary faith, always seeking to bring in new believers. Other faiths, like Judaism, are not. It is the faith of a mother that determines the Jewishness of her offspring. Some Jews would argue that it is impossible for a non-Jew (a Gentile) to convert to the faith however, all branches of Judaism allow conversion.

Some religious leaders clearly have more influence than others. The Pope, for example, leads the world's 1000 million Roman Catholics. Although he is advised by bishops and other Church leaders, he has the authority to speak on occasions with the voice of God. When he does so, he is said to be speaking 'ex cathedra' (with full authority) and his words become part of the Church's teaching.

Religious institutions have a considerable influence within the different religions. In Buddhism, the sangha is the assembly of monks that was founded by the Buddha himself. A daily Buddhist recitation is 'I go to the sangha for refuge.' The Khalsa, containing men and women, is the ruling body of Sikhism, which was formed by Guru Gobind Singh in 1699. Committed Sikhs are initiated into this fellowship through a ceremony that involves the use of amrit (symbolic sugared water).

IMPORTANT WORDS

Easter; Christian festival celebrating the resurrection of Christ
Holy Communion; Christian service remembering the death of Christ
Imam; leader of prayers in a mosque
Passover; Jewish festival celebrating the release of the early Jews from Egyptian slavery
Rabbi; title given to an authorised teacher in a synagogue
Shabbat; (Sabbath) the day of rest each Friday evening to Saturday evening for Jews

Tasks

1. Give **TWO** reasons why tradition is so important in all religions.

2. a. What was the Exodus?
   b. During which festival is the Exodus celebrated by Jews each year?
   c. Why is the Exodus still important for Jews today?

3. a. Which two churches trace their origins back to the earliest years of Christianity?
   b. Why do you think it is important for them to do this?

4. Give **THREE** reasons why religious leaders are so important in most of the world's religions.

SUMMARY

1. Traditions play a very important part in religious worship and believers try to enter into them through worship as if they were happening today.

2. Religious leaders play an important part in religious worship. They lead people in worship and explain the meaning of religious faith. In some religions they act as a bridge between God and the worshipper.

3. Some religious leaders play a very important role in modern life. The most powerful modern religious leader is the Pope who is the leader of the world's Roman Catholics. Occasionally he is believed to speak with the authority of God.

▼ Many Christians believe that there is a direct line between bishops today and the disciples of Jesus. God's authority has been passed down from one to the other through the 'laying-on of hands' over the centuries.

TRUTH AND SPIRITUALITY

1:6 Faith communities and voluntary organisations

What are faith communities and why are they important in the search for religious truth?

Most religious people belong to a faith community of some kind. It is most likely to be their local place of worship where they meet and pray with other believers. For most people, this is an important part of their spiritual journey. Others, though, feel that they have been 'called' to dedicate themselves to God in a special way. These people are said to have a 'vocation', a word often used to describe those who become priests, monks or nuns. The word is particularly used in a Christian context where people often speak of these vocations as 'callings'.

Monastic communities

Within three centuries of the death of Jesus, many Christians were leaving their home and family to live in the desert. There they gave themselves to a life of holy reading, thought and prayer. To begin with they lived on their own, but they soon started to form communities with other like-minded people. These communities began to draw up strict rules for their members. The most important was the Rule of St Benedict, in the sixth century CE, which demanded that each monk live a life of poverty, obedience and chastity. These three demands soon spread to govern the lives of everyone living in monasteries. Communities of women, living in convents, later adopted the same Rule. It is still in place today.

▼ Christian monks and nuns give themselves to a life of prayer and service to others.

Christianity has a strong monastic tradition. There are many different monastic orders with most of them coming from a Roman Catholic background. The commitment expected of those who join a monastery or a convent is lifelong. Monks and nuns are also an important part of Buddhism, although they are not expected to remain in their monastic order for the rest of their lives. In Hinduism, people may choose to spend time in an ashram (a religious community) gathered around a guru – a spiritual teacher.

Other Christian communities

There are also interdenominational Christian communities in which the demands on those who belong are rather different. People can belong to these without giving up their ordinary employment. The community centred on Iona, in Scotland, for instance, expects its members to meet together for just a week each year and to spend the rest of the time in their own locality. They do, however, stay in contact in other ways. They can put the principles of the Iona community – emphasising the importance of prayer, study and service – into practice in their everyday lives. In this way, they are a witness to the Christian message wherever they are. They are also expected to give one-tenth of their money, called a 'tithe', to further the work of the community.

Voluntary organisations

Serving other people is an important part of religious faith. Many do this by working through their local worship group and reaching out to help those in the community around. Others belong to voluntary organisations that have a religious basis, which they support through their gifts and prayers. Many Christians, for instance, channel their support through such organisations as Christian Aid, Jews through the Jewish National Fund and Muslims through Muslim Aid. Other organisations work to help the homeless, the poor, young people, people with AIDS and people in prison. The Salvation Army, for example, does all these things, as well as running a tracing service for those who have left home without letting relatives know where they are.

> *I was hungry and you fed me, thirsty and you gave me a drink; I was a stranger and you received me in your homes, naked and you clothed me; I was sick and you took care of me, in prison and you visited me. ... whenever you did this for one of the least important of these members of my family, you did it for me.*
>
> **... THE BIBLE (MATTHEW 25.35–40)**

▲ In the Buddhist tradition, monks (like these shown) and nuns are supported by the gifts of ordinary believers.

> *A monk was asked, "What do you do there in the monastery?" He replied. "We fall and get up, we fall and get up, fall and get up again."*

... THE WAY OF THE MONK, CHRISTIAN BOOK

All religions stress that it is the duty of believers to meet the needs of the less fortunate members of society. There is a close link between what a person believes and what they do. As one of the writers in the New Testament wrote: "Show me your faith without deeds and I will show you my faith by what I do." (James 2.18)

Tasks

1. Why did Christians form monastic communities in the first place?
2. What is the Rule of St Benedict and what does it expect of all monks and nuns?
3. Write about **THREE** different kinds of religious community.
4. Explain what part voluntary organisations play for many people as part of their religious faith.
5. Why do you think that people decide to live in a monastic community? Give reasons for your answer.

 Think about ...

The desert has always been looked upon as a place for prayer and reflection. Why do you think that many people over the centuries have spent their lives there looking for God?

IMPORTANT WORDS

Guru; a holy man or spiritual teacher in Indian religions, especially Hinduism and Sikhism

Salvation Army; Christian organisation that spends time helping the poor and needy

SUMMARY

1 Most religious people belong to a faith community based on their local place of worship.

2 Monastic communities have played an important part in Christianity and Buddhism for centuries. Christian monks and nuns follow the rule of poverty, obedience and chastity.

3 Many people belong to voluntary organisations that bring help to people in many different kinds of need. Some of these organisations have religious foundations.

TRUTH AND SPIRITUALITY

1:7 Religious worship

Why is worship such an important part of religious faith?

Much of a person's religious faith is to do with the way that they feel about God and about themselves. As religious feelings are often amongst the deepest that people have, they need to find an outlet for them. It is through acts of worship that people try to express their feelings about God, themselves and other people. Most acts of worship take place within a religious or faith community, although individual acts of worship and piety (holy activity) are also encouraged.

The faith communities in which acts of worship take place are often likened to a family. Christians, for instance, often speak of the 'church family'. As with most families, a church looks after the needs of all its members, providing loving help and support when this is needed.

Religious worship

> *Everyone has the right to freedom of thought, conscience and religion; this right includes freedom to change his religion or belief, and freedom, either alone or in community with others and in public or private, to manifest his religion or belief in teaching, practice, worship and observance.*
>
> ... **UNITED NATIONS UNIVERSAL DECLARATION OF HUMAN RIGHTS, ARTICLE 18**

As the United Nations Declaration of Human Rights makes clear, every man and woman has the basic human right to take part in acts of worship and to change their religion at any time, whether they make their decision known to others or not. They also have the right to teach their religious faith to their children and others, and to practise that faith and worship openly.

Religious worship can take many different forms. It can take place inside or outside a place of worship. It can be highly organised or spontaneous. It can involve many people or take the form of silent and solitary meditation. It can take place in a simple building like a Quaker Meeting House or in a beautiful building, such as a cathedral. It can make use of a variety of special symbols, such as a rosary or a tefillin or not, depending on the taste and needs of the worshippers. Religious worship is rich and varied, taking many forms.

Problems of worship

Religious worship is not easy. God is a Spirit and human beings are material. God is totally beyond human reach. The words that people use in their worship are often taken from everyday life and so are inadequate to describe spiritual truths. This is why people have always needed holy objects to help them to worship God. Religions recognise this, but they have also warned about its dangers. Islam, for instance, will not allow any representation of God, animals or human beings in its mosques. The traditional teaching from Muhammad onwards is that the danger of idolatry (worshipping the object rather than the reality behind it) is too real and so has to be avoided.

▼ The Christian religion allows for a wide variety of worship to meet the needs of different people. Here people attend a Protestant church in China.

One of the Ten Commandments, at the heart of Judaism, forbids any statue to be made to represent God. On the other hand, such statues (called 'murtis') are at the heart of Hinduism. The statues represent an aspect of the personality of God, not God as a person. As long as Hindu worshippers remember this, they will not confuse the image with the reality towards which it is pointing.

> *God is Spirit, and only by the power of His spirit can people worship him as he really is.*
>
> ... **THE BIBLE (JOHN 4.24)**

Belonging to a worshipping community

For the majority of religious believers, belonging to a worshipping community is an essential part of their religious experience. It provides them with:

- pastoral support – this simply means that it gives them support to live as a religious believer and as a human being
- the opportunity to express their faith in terms of worship; worship is a communal experience
- the opportunity to live a lifestyle in keeping with their religious faith
- a means of serving others, both in the religious community and in the wider society
- the opportunity to witness to their faith and, in the case of religions like Christianity and Islam, to witness to the wider community and make converts.

 Think about ...

Do people have a basic human right to believe and worship as they please?
Think of **ONE** reason to support your answer.
Why might someone disagree with this?

IMPORTANT WORDS

Meditation; a spiritual discipline used in many religions involving stilling the mind

Quakers; Christian society, which began in England in the 1600s

Tasks

1. a. What are people trying to express when they take part in an act of worship?
   b. Why do you think that acts of worship are important to so many people?
2. Can you think of **TWO** ways in which belonging to a religious community, such as a church, is rather like belonging to a family?
3. a. Write down **FOUR** ways in which religious worship might express itself.
   b. What do you think might be the main difficulty for many people who wish to take part in an act of worship?

SUMMARY

1 Acts of worship are an essential part of belonging to a religion for most people.

2 Through worship people express their feelings about God. It is a basic human right that people should have the freedom to worship as they wish.

3 Religious worship can never be easy because God is a Spirit and human language will always be inadequate to express spiritual truths.

▼ An act of Sikh worship. Men and women worship together, although they sit separately.

TRUTH AND SPIRITUALITY

1:8 Religious symbols

What part do symbols play in the search for religious truth?

Symbols play a very important part in religious worship. God is believed to be so great that He cannot, in normal circumstances, be known by human beings. He is beyond all human experience and language. Many people feel that God can be partly understood, and experienced, through the use of symbols. These symbols can only reveal, at best, part of the truth.

■ CHRISTIANITY

The use of symbols in Christian worship is a good illustration of this. At the heart of Holy Communion – the most important Christian service – stand the symbols of bread and wine. Through using these symbols during the service, Christians can begin to enter into the meaning and importance of the death and resurrection of Jesus. Another Christian symbol – that of the cross – is also widely used for this purpose. There are crosses visible in most churches, with one often sited above the altar, the holiest part of a church. In the services of infant and believers' baptism the symbol of water is used to highlight the importance of spiritual washing and new life. There are many other Christian symbols that are also an important part of worship and devotion.

■ JUDAISM

The Jewish way of life is full of symbols. They include the important dietary laws (kashrut) which symbolise the cleanliness and obedience that God expects from all Jews. The laws may not have an obvious meaning, but their real significance lies in the obedience to God and His laws. The mezuzah is an important symbol to Jews of God's presence within the home whilst, in the synagogue, the Everlasting Light reassures them of God's eternal presence with them.

■ ISLAM

The crescent moon and a star are the basic symbols of Islam. The shape and design of the mosque are full of reminders of Allah. The four minarets and the dome remind worshippers of the all-important Five Pillars of Islam. These are the five beliefs that are at the heart of the faith, a belief in: Allah, prayer five times a day, giving money to help the poor, fasting during the month of Ramadan, and a pilgrimage (called the Hajj) to Makkah.

> *There is no god except Allah, Muhammad is the Messenger of Allah.*
>
> **... THE SHAHADAH, THE MUSLIM STATEMENT OF FAITH**

▲ The cross is a very important Christian symbol, pointing worshippers to the death of Jesus on the cross.

■ Hinduism

The most important Hindu symbols are the statues of the gods. They are not themselves objects of worship but they do point worshippers to the Supreme Spirit, Brahman. Another important Hindu symbol is the sacred syllable – AUM. The three sounds of the sacred syllable are believed to contain all the secrets of the universe. It is spoken before reading the scriptures, prayer, meditation or any act of worship.

■ Sikhism

There are many important symbols in Sikhism including the Five Ks, which are worn by every member of the Khalsa. Each of the Five Ks are important symbols of Sikh identity – uncut hair (kesh), a comb (kangha), a steel band worn on the right wrist (kara), a pair of shorts (kachs) and a short sword (khanda).

By using symbols, worshippers are reminded of important aspects of their faith. Symbols allow people to focus on their faith in a way that would otherwise be impossible.

Tasks

1. a. Explain why religious symbols are useful and important for those who are offering worship.
   b. Write down **THREE** religious symbols taken from any of the religions you have studied and explain what they symbolise.
2. The important thing about a symbol is that it is not, in itself, the object of worship but points to a spiritual reality. Why do you think it is important for a religion to stress this?
3. 'It is perfectly possible to worship God without using any symbols.' Argue for or against this statement.

IMPORTANT WORDS

Believer's baptism;	baptismal service for adults held in a Baptist church
Infant baptism;	baptismal service for infants held in Roman Catholic and Anglican churches
Khalsa;	the Sikh fellowship of committed males and females
Makkah;	birthplace of Muhammad and spiritual centre of Islam
Ramadan;	ninth month of Muslim calendar, observed as a time of fasting

▲ The flag flying from the gurdwara is a visible symbol of the Sikh presence in the community.

SUMMARY

1 Symbols are a very important part of religious worship. They have a meaning and represent something.

2 The most important Christian symbols are the bread and wine of Holy Communion and the cross. They point to the death of Jesus. Water is another important Christian symbol.

3 The dietary laws, the mezuzah and the Everlasting Light are important Jewish symbols. The crescent moon and star and the minarets of the mosque are important Muslim symbols.

4 There are important symbols in Hinduism and Sikhism, which point to the central beliefs of the faiths.

TRUTH AND SPIRITUALITY

1:9 Religious piety

Why are prayer and meditation such important parts of the religious experience and search for truth?

Prayer and meditation are extremely important parts of the religious experience. They are to be found, in one form or another, in every religion. Prayer is the way that worshippers make contact with God or, in the case of Buddhism, the way that they seek spiritual enlightenment within. Prayers may be spoken aloud but, just as likely, they are 'spoken' silently within a person's heart (spiritual being). This silent prayer is called 'meditation' and is particularly important in Buddhism, although other religions also use it. Meditation is often prompted by thinking deeply about an object or a mantra (a special religious chant).

Some people, such as monks and nuns, devote themselves to a lifetime of prayer. The majority of religious believers, though, fit it into a busy daily life.

Prayer

> *When you pray, go into your room, close the door, and pray to your Father, who is unseen. And your Father, who sees what you do in private, will reward you openly.*
>
> **... THE BIBLE (MATTHEW 6.6)**

Except for Buddhist believers, people who pray are usually:

- worshipping God by showing their devotion and respect
- confessing their sins (wrongdoings) to God
- asking God to help and bless others
- asking for God's help in their own lives.

Some kind of preparation is often thought to be necessary before a person can pray. Muslims, for instance, remove their shoes and wash thoroughly before they pray. This washing ritual is called 'wudu'. Hindus and Sikhs also remove their shoes before going into their places of worship. Jewish men often drape their tallit (prayer shawl) around their shoulders and wear their tefillin before they pray. These actions are carried out because they are thought to be the appropriate things to do in the presence of God – and to show their respect for the Almighty.

Confession and thanksgiving

There is often room in prayer for people to confess their sins. In the Roman Catholic Church this has traditionally taken the form of the person confessing their sins to God through a priest. This has been thought to be particularly important before taking Holy Communion at Easter. Worshippers also come into the presence of God to offer their praise. Thanksgiving is a very important part of prayer. In the Jewish faith, for instance, there is said to be a prayer to cover everything for which someone might wish to be thankful!

▼ Prayer has been described as the most basic of all religious activities and can take place anywhere.

Intercession

Some people think that praying is a selfish business, with people concerned only about themselves and their own problems. Real praying, though, will include praying for others and all religions emphasise this. This kind of prayer is called 'intercession'. Praying for others, known and unknown, draws worshippers together. This often happens after a national disaster. Christian leaders reported that churches were much fuller than usual after the events in New York on 11 September 2001. People often turn to God when they are faced with enormous challenges and are very worried about the future. It is an acknowledgement that the problems are too big for human beings to solve on their own without some kind of divine assistance.

Discipline and mysticism

Many people feel that they need to pray within a physical discipline. Yoga is one way for people to impose this discipline upon themselves and both Hindus and Christians sometimes use this. For them there is a strong link between physical discipline and prayer and meditation. For a few this can lead to mysticism. This is the belief in the attainment, through contemplation or self-surrender, of truths that are inaccessible to the understanding or the intellect. A few believe that such mysticism can lead to the possibility of a spiritual unity with God.

▲ Although meditation is a very important Buddhist activity, it is also used in other religions.

Tasks

1. a. What is prayer?
   b. Why do you think that people pray?
   c. What is meditation?
2. Read what Jesus had to say about prayer *(see quotation)*. Put this into your own words. What do you think is the important point that he was making about prayer?
3. a. What are the important aspects of prayer?
   b. How do people from different religions prepare themselves for prayer?

 Think about ...

- Do you believe that it might be possible to contact a Supreme Being (God) through prayer? Give **TWO** reasons for your answer.
- Are you surprised that people often turn to prayer when they feel under threat? Give **ONE** reason for your answer.

IMPORTANT WORDS

Mantra; term used in Hinduism, Sikhism and Buddhism for a sacred formula or chant

Roman Catholic Church; the community of Christians that owes its allegiance to the Pope

SUMMARY

1. The activity of prayer is common to all religions.

2. In most religions prayer involves worshipping, confession, seeking help for oneself and for others and thanksgiving.

3. In most religions, certain actions and ways of dressing are thought to be appropriate for prayer. They are used to show that prayer is special and different from everyday activities.

TRUTH AND SPIRITUALITY

1:10 The creative spirit

What is the creative spirit and why has it played such an important part in spirituality?

Spiritual truth is found in many different places. For centuries people have turned to holy books and spiritual leaders for enlightenment. Some people have found help and guidance by giving themselves to a life of prayer and service in a faith community. Various religious symbols help many to pray and worship. These are 'traditional' paths to spiritual truth. Over the centuries, though, others have tried to express their spirituality in more unusual ways by bringing their own particular gifts and skills to their worship of God. This has often allowed others to celebrate and share the skills of those with a 'creative spirit'.

> *Artists in a way are religious anyhow. They have to be, if by 'religious' one means believing that life has some significance, and some meaning, which is what I think it means. An artist couldn't work without believing that.*
>
> **... HENRY MOORE, SCULPTOR**

The creative spirit

Wherever there has been religion, men and women have wanted to express their faith through their own gifts and skills as writers, artists, sculptors or poets. Religion has always inspired creative men and women. Sometimes they have produced works of art that have been inspired by religious themes taken from their faith. The life of Jesus and incidents from the Gospels, for instance, have inspired many artists. The birth and death of Jesus, in particular, have inspired some great works of art. Sometimes such creative skills have been used directly in worship. A good example of this is the use of icons, special religious paintings, which are widely used by Greek Orthodox Christians, and others, as part of their worship. The finished article is an offering made by the artist to God as part of their own worship.

In some religions, great and beautiful buildings have been dedicated to the worship of God. Amongst them are cathedrals, although many churches are equally beautiful on a smaller scale. The Christian tradition has always been that nothing is too beautiful or costly for the worship of God. In both Christianity and Islam there is the teaching that skilled craftsmen can do no better with their craft than to dedicate that skill to God in building a beautiful place of worship.

▼ Muslims who take part in building a mosque are promised a place in paradise after they die. The Dome of the Rock, shown here, is in Jerusalem and was built in 687CE.

▲ Churches often contain striking examples of religious art. The Sistine Chapel, in the Vatican, contains a painting by Michelangelo of the Last Judgement.

The creative spirit has also shown itself elsewhere over the centuries. Great works of literature; wonderful pieces of music; beautiful stained-glass windows; moving dances and pieces of drama have helped people to worship. These creative activities have done two things:

1. They have provided the opportunity for talented people to express how they feel about God.
2. They have helped millions of other people understand truths about God and themselves that they would not have appreciated otherwise.

 Not everything has a name. Some things lead us into the realm beyond words. Art thaws even the frozen, darkened soul, opening it to lofty spiritual experience. Through Art we are sometimes sent revelations which cannot be achieved in any other way.

... ALEKSANDR SOLZHENITSYN, RUSSIAN AUTHOR

Tasks

1. Write down what you understand by the phrase 'the creative spirit'.
2. According to Henry Moore, what is it that every artist must believe before they can produce a real work of art?
3. Read the comment by Aleksandr Solzhenitsyn and explain why he thinks that art is so important.
4. Give an example of art being used directly in religious worship.

❗ Think about ...

Visit a local place of worship, look at a work of art, listen to a beautiful piece of music or do something similar. Try to work out how someone might look at or listen to that work of art and be inspired. Talk to other people, in your group, to see if you all received the same 'message' from it.

✓ Exam tip

There is no reason why in an exam answer you should not refer to a work of art that really appeals to you – such as a building, a painting or a piece of music. Ensure it is relevant to the question. In all exam answers, relevance is the key – make sure you answer the question being asked.

SUMMARY

1. Over the centuries people have expressed their feelings about God through art, literature, architecture, music, poetry and by other means. The religious traditions have, in the main, encouraged this although some religions have been very conscious of the dangers of so doing.

2. Religion has been a great sponsor of the arts over the centuries, to the great benefit of worshippers.

TRUTH AND SPIRITUALITY

1:11 Truth and spirituality in Christianity

What do Christians believe about truth and spirituality?

Christians believe that God is the truth. The Gospels record the words of Jesus: "I am the way, the truth and the life." (John 14.6) The Gospels also tell us that Jesus promised his followers that, after his departure from the earth, they would be given the companionship of the Holy Spirit – who would guide them all into truth. Christians believe that the spiritual truth that they seek is to be found in the three members of the Trinity – God the Father, God the Son and God the Holy Spirit. The Christian Trinity can be known and experienced through the Scriptures. They are God's repository of truth.

You will know the truth and the truth will set you free.

... THE BIBLE (JOHN 8.32)

Truth

Most Christians belong to a church and this is part of the worldwide Christian Church. The Church has a big influence on what the vast majority of Christians believe and how they behave. For Roman Catholics there are three sources of truth – the Pope, the teachings and traditions of the Church and the Bible. Other Christians and Protestants do not recognise any human authority beneath God. For most Protestants, Christian tradition is not as important in their search for the truth as the Bible. They see the Bible as the word of God.

At the end of the fourth century, the Christian Church officially combined the scriptures of Judaism with their own holy books to form the Bible. Roman Catholics believe that the Church alone is able to understand and interpret the Bible. Protestants believe that individual Christians can hear God speaking to them through the Bible without any other help. Roman Catholics look to the Church and the Bible for the truth. Protestants look to the Bible alone. This is the basic difference between these two great branches of the Christian Church.

Spirituality

There are two sides to Christian spirituality that are important to remember.
1. Much Christian spirituality centres around the life and worship of the Church. For the vast majority of Christians the most important act of worship is Holy Communion – a service that has different names in the various Churches. The bread and wine are the basic symbols, which are used to enter into, and celebrate, the death and resurrection of Jesus; this is at the centre of Christian spirituality.

   Celebrating Holy Communion is the most important spiritual experience for the majority of Christians. Two Churches, the Salvation Army and the Quakers, do not celebrate Holy Communion or any of the special services, called 'sacraments', which are so important in many Churches.

   Away from public worship, spirituality is also developed individually. Most Christians, for instance, maintain a regular prayer and Bible-reading routine. In their prayers, Orthodox Christians often use an icon to help them, whilst many Roman Catholics use a rosary.

2. There is a close link between Christian spirituality and action in the community. In Britain, and elsewhere, the Church has been actively engaged in social activity for centuries. The Church has been and is actively involved in feeding the hungry; housing the homeless; clothing those without a regular income and helping those involved in drug and alcohol abuse. The motivation for this activity is the teaching of Jesus when he said that those who help the needy are doing their act of charity to him – even if they do not realise it. (Matthew 25.31–46)

The time is coming and is already here, when by the power of God's Spirit people will worship the Father as he really is, offering him the true worship that he wants. God is a spirit and only by the power of his Spirit can people worship him as he really is.

... THE BIBLE (JOHN 4.23)

Tasks

1. How do Roman Catholics and Protestant Christians differ in the way that they understand the truth and the sources of truth?
2. What do many Christians believe about the Bible and the truth?
3. What part does the church and individual devotion play in Christian spirituality?
4. What is the link between Christian spirituality and action to help people in need?

IMPORTANT WORDS

Icon; an image of Christ, the Virgin Mary or a saint
Sacrament; an outward, visible sign of an inward, spiritual blessing conveyed through a special church service
Trinity; the Christian belief that there is one God in three persons – God the Father, God the Son and God the Holy Spirit

SUMMARY

1 Christians believe that the truth is found in God the Father, the Son and the Holy Spirit – the Trinity.

2 The Bible contains the truth about God. It plays a very important part in public worship and private devotions.

3 Christian spirituality grows through involvement with a church and involves social action to meet human need.

▼ Much of Christian spirituality centres around the value and importance of prayer.

TRUTH AND SPIRITUALITY

1:12 Truth and spirituality in Judaism and Islam

What do Jews and Muslims believe about truth and spirituality?

Judaism and Islam are monotheistic religions. This means that they both believe in one God. This affects the way in which they approach truth and spirituality.

■ JUDAISM

Truth

For Jews, their scriptures (the Tanakh) are the ultimate source of authority and truth. They were written over a long period of time and accepted as authoritative just before the end of the first century CE. They are made up of three parts – the books of the Law, the books of the Prophets and the Writings. The books of the Law, the Torah, are the most important of these. The five books of the Torah contain everything that is important about the Jewish way of life – circumcision, dietary laws, the Sabbath day, the Ten Commandments and much more. They also contain the early history of the Jewish people. It is there that spiritual truth is to be found. There are also other holy books, such as the Talmud, which contain Jewish wisdom from over the centuries and which are regularly consulted by Jews today.

Spirituality

> *Remember the sabbath day and keep it holy. Six days you shall labour ... but the seventh day is a sabbath of the LORD your God ... . For in six days the LORD made heaven and earth and sea, and all that is in them, and He rested the seventh day; therefore the LORD blessed the sabbath day and hallowed it.*
>
> **... THE TANAKH (EXODUS 20.8–11)**

Jews show their commitment to God by keeping to the traditions of the faith, observing the festivals that commemorate important events in Jewish history and treasuring the Sabbath day as a day of rest. There is an old Jewish saying that 'more than Israel having kept the Sabbath, the Sabbath has kept Israel'. The Sabbath day is at the heart of Jewish spirituality. Keeping it as a day of rest is a very important spiritual discipline. It allows the body and spirit to recover before the week of work ahead. Jews believe that it was instituted after God had spent six days creating the world – when He rested on the seventh.

▲ The Torah scroll contains the teachings at the heart of Judaism.

■ ISLAM

Truth

The Shahadah tells all Muslims that there are two principles to the truth:

- There is no God but Allah.
- Muhammad is the Prophet of Allah.

This, for a Muslim, is the basis of all truth. It is also the basis of the Qur'an, the Muslim holy book, which is the word of God. The Qur'an is not open to discussion or debate and its teachings have to be accepted without question by all Muslims.

Spirituality

Islamic spirituality is based on the Five Pillars, since these are the foundation on which the faith is built. A Muslim must accept not only the Shahadah, but also the importance of prayer in daily life; an obligation to give 2.5 per cent of their income to the poor; to undertake fasting during the month of Ramadan each year and make an obligation to undertake a pilgrimage, called the Hajj, to Makkah once in a lifetime. An important factor in Muslim spirituality is that each believer must account for their life to Allah on the Day of Judgement.

> *... celebrate the praises of thy Lord before the rising of the sun, and before its setting; yea, celebrate them for part of the hours of the night, and at the sides of the day.*
>
> **... THE QUR'AN (20.130)**

▲ Prayers, five times a day, are at the heart of Muslim spirituality.

! Think about ...

What do you think the saying that 'more than Israel keeping the Sabbath, the Sabbath has kept Israel' means?

Tasks

1.a. What is the Sabbath day?
  b. What is the main reason for Jews keeping the Sabbath day?
2. Write about the Tanakh, explaining what it is and why it is important.
3.a. What are the two sides to the truth in Islam?
  b. How must Muslims treat the Qur'an?
4.a. What are the Five Pillars?
  b. What do they say?

IMPORTANT WORDS

Hajj; pilgrimage of Muslims to the holy city of Makkah
Shahadah; the Muslim statement of belief in Allah and Muhammad
Tanakh; Jewish term for their Scriptures

SUMMARY

1 For Jews, their Scriptures are the most important guide to the truth. In them they discover what God expects from the Jewish people. Jewish spirituality centres on the traditions of the faith and especially the keeping of the Sabbath day.

2 For Muslims, the truth is found in the Qur'an and compounded in the Five Pillars and especially the Shahadah. These are also the basis of Muslim spirituality, with their emphasis on prayer, giving to the poor, fasting and pilgrimage.

TRUTH AND SPIRITUALITY

1:13 Truth and spirituality in Hinduism, Sikhism and Buddhism

How are truth and spirituality expressed in Hinduism, Sikhism and Buddhism?

HINDUISM

Truth for the Hindu stems from a belief in one God, Brahman, who is known in the world in many different forms. Everything came from Brahman in the beginning and all Hindus hope, after many rebirths, to be absorbed back into God. There are many paths that can be taken to achieve this and sadhus (holy men) and gurus (spiritual teachers) have chosen their own paths.

Most Hindus, though, have chosen to follow the path of personal devotion and worship. This worship, called 'puja', is concentrated on the home, where there is a shrine to the family god. In the Bhagavad Gita the god Krishna said he would accept any sacrifice – whether a leaf, fruit or water. The only condition is that it must be offered with love. Each day, fresh offerings are placed in front of the god and prayers are said. It is the mother in a Hindu family who takes most of the responsibility for encouraging the spiritual growth of members of her family. Visits may be made to the mandir to worship but these are not considered to be essential.

SIKHISM

Sikhs worship one God, Nam, who cannot be understood, since Nam is beyond human reach. In the Guru Granth Sahib, God is described as Eternal Truth (the True Guru) and this is the most important description of God. The ten gurus, including Guru Nanak, were the human representatives of Nam on earth. The final Guru is the holy book, the Guru Granth Sahib. This is the complete revelation of God's truth and is the symbol of God's presence on earth. As such, it is far more important than a human guru can be.

Sikhs begin each day by reciting a part of the Guru Granth Sahib. This is the Mool Mantra, the basic statement of Sikh belief. Sikhs also spend time in the gurdwara listening to the Guru Granth Sahib being read. Just listening to the sound of its words is spiritually beneficial. At the conclusion of this service, time is spent in the langar eating a specially prepared meal. This is a very old tradition, going back to the Gurus, expressing the unity that is at the heart of Sikh spirituality. Many Sikhs also belong to the Khalsa, a fellowship that unites all those committed to the faith.

BUDDHISM

> *Spirituality I take to be concerned with those qualities of the human spirit – such as love and compassion, a sense of responsibility, a sense of harmony – which bring happiness to both self and others.*
>
> ... DALAI LAMA, A TIBETAN BUDDHIST LEADER

Buddhism is different from the other religions in this book. Buddhists do not believe in god. They believe that each person is undertaking their own search for the truth with the Buddha as their main guide. Buddhists turn to the teachings of the Buddha and the teachings of monks and nuns who can help them.

Buddhist spirituality is built around meditation. Often the statue of the Buddha acts as a focus for this. Worshippers make their offerings of flowers, incense or food to express their devotion to the Buddha before they meditate. They also use spiritual chants (mantras) to help concentrate their mind. In Tibet, mantras are put into prayer wheels and spun around to send out positive vibrations to everyone who hears them.

IMPORTANT WORDS

Guru Nanak;	the first Sikh Guru and the founder of Sikhism
Mandir;	Hindu temple where the images of God is housed
Mool Mantra;	statement of Sikh belief from opening of Guru Granth Sahib
Puja;	reverence and worship in Hinduism and Buddhism
Sadhu;	Hindu holy man

Tasks

1. a. What is the spiritual goal of every Hindu?
   b. How do most Hindus try to reach this goal?
   c. What did the god Krishna say about true worship?
2. a. Where do Sikhs look for the complete revelation of god's truth?
   b. What is the Guru Granth Sahib and why is it so important to the Sikh in their search for the truth?
   c. What is the langar in the gurdwara and why is it important to Sikh spirituality?
3. a. What do Buddhists believe to be the goal of all spiritual activity and meditation?
   b. What is a mantra and how do some Buddhists use them in their quest for spiritual enlightenment?

Exam tip
It is important to realise that both Hindus and Sikhs express their spiritual goal in terms of God, while Buddhists are concerned to reach internal enlightenment. There is a real difference in spiritual objectives. You must be able to show that you understand this distinction.

SUMMARY

1 There are many spiritual paths that Hindus can take but the most popular is that of personal devotion to the family god.

2 Sikh spirituality is based upon the Guru Granth Sahib, the final revelation of God's truth.

3 Buddhist spirituality is centred on the teachings of the Buddha and the quest for personal enlightenment.

▼ Prayer wheels are an important part of devotion in Tibetan Buddhism.

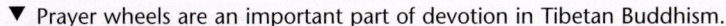

TRUTH AND SPIRITUALITY

Exam help ...

In this chapter you have looked at the nature of truth and spirituality. You have discovered that truth comes in many different forms – including scientific, historical and religious truth. Mention of religious truth reminds us that all religions teach that human beings are more than just a body – they are a spirit. Faith is very important in the search for spiritual truth and fulfilment. The holy books, religious traditions, membership of the faith community and religious worship all play a part in the spiritual search.

1.a. Give **ONE** example of a holy book.
b. What do religious people mean by the word 'conscience'?
c. How does science prove that something is true?
d. What do religious believers gain from their membership of a worshipping community?

1.a. Any recognised holy scriptures – the Bible, the Tanakh, the Qur'an, the Guru Granth Sahib, the Vedas ... will do for this answer.
b. The importance of the conscience to religious believers/the voice of God/upbringing/moral standards that were taught by parents, school, religious place of worship/that which is known to be right and truthful/can be followed or rejected/a bad conscience.
c. Scientific truth is based on observation and proof/experimentation/ability to repeat the experiment and obtain the same result at any time/science is never fixed/based on observation and evidence at the time/evidence may be interpreted differently by people/new evidence may lead to a change of view.
d. Nature of faith communities/pastoral support/teaching/communal worship/meeting with like-minded people/corporate witness to community/importance in the lives of most religious believers/strength to be gained from association with others.

2.a. What is truth?
b. What is spirituality?

2.a. Different types of truth:
- scientific truth – dependent on experimentation and careful observation of evidence.
- historical truth – uses sciences, such as archaeology, to increase historical information/use of documentary evidence/information can change understanding of historical events.
- spiritual and moral truth – link of religious truth with faith, sometimes moral and religious truths come from the same source, sometimes they are separate.

b. A wide idea to embrace traditional and non-traditional approaches to spirituality/the former will embrace holy books, prayer and meditation, acts of worship, visits to holy places, involvement in a faith community/the latter will include anything that brings an element of awe including music, beauty, art, architecture and so on.

3. Why is the use of symbols so important in the search for religious truth? You must only refer to TWO religions.

3. Importance of symbols in religion/God so great that He can only be partly understood through the use of symbols/worship impossible without symbols.
- Christianity – bread and wine at Holy Communion, the cross, water in the services of infant and believer's baptism.
- Judaism full of symbols – kashrut, mezuzah, Everlasting Light.
- Muslim symbols – crescent and star, minarets and dome.
- Khalsa symbols in Sikhism.

CHAPTER 2
Matters of life

To make real sense of the issues covered in this chapter, you should be aware of the implications of asking three basic questions about life itself and the teachings of the different religions on each question.

When does human life begin?

Does it begin when a baby is conceived? Is it after a certain number of weeks, possibly when all of the baby's organs begin to grow? Is it when, as some religions teach, the soul takes up residence in the body? Could it be when the baby is able to survive separately from its mother – around 23 weeks of pregnancy? Is it when the baby is born?

Many of the issues discussed in this chapter depend on the answer given to this question. It is a matter of considerable significance to the world's religions.

Is there such a thing as pre-existence?

Three religions – Hinduism, Sikhism and Buddhism – teach that there is. Three religions – Christianity, Judaism and Islam – say that there is not. If people believe that we go through the cycle of birth, life and death many times, then this has important implications for the way we understand such modern issues as genetic engineering and cloning.

Who is responsible for life?

Apart from Buddhism, the main religions all insist that God is the creator and sustainer of all forms of life, especially human life. God is there at the very beginning when life begins with a fertilised ovum and God alone can determine when each life will end. If God is not the creator of life, then who is? This leads us to wonder what part doctors and parents should play in deciding the issues that are discussed in this chapter.

These questions are raised in the discussions ahead. You will need to understand the relevance of your answers to them, in connection with the issue being discussed and also in connection with the teachings of the different religions. You will become aware of the problems of applying the teachings of ancient holy books to modern issues. In some cases, religions are only just beginning to appreciate the challenges that some of these issues offer to traditional faith.

Recent developments in medicine and medical research raise major ethical, moral and religious issues. Whether religions can continue to base their responses to them on their holy books alone remains to be seen.

MATTERS OF LIFE

2:1 The beginning of life

When does human life begin?

> *Life must be protected with the utmost care from the moment of conception (since that is when life begins).*
>
> ... ROMAN CATHOLIC DOCUMENT, GAUDIUM ET SPES

A human being takes nine months to develop in the womb of its mother. It starts life as a zygote (a just-fertilised ovum), becomes a blastocyst, then at 14 days it is implanted in the wall of the uterus. It then becomes an embryo. After eight weeks the essential organs begin to grow and it is called a 'foetus'. Its organs will continue to grow throughout the pregnancy.

When does life begin?

This is a very difficult question to answer. There are five possible answers.

1. **At conception.** This is the belief of the Catholic Church. It teaches that a genetically unique individual comes into existence the moment the ovum is fertilised by the sperm. The fertilised ovum takes half of its genetic make-up from its mother and half from its father.

2. **At the blastocyst stage.** As many as 50 per cent of all fertilised ova are lost through miscarriages (spontaneous or natural abortions) early in the pregnancy as the fertilised egg fails to implant itself in the wall of the uterus. Soon after the blastocyst stage a pregnancy can be confirmed and a woman knows that she is going to become a mother.

3. **When the embryo becomes a spiritual being.** This is the traditional religious teaching. The Talmud, an important Jewish holy book, teaches that this happens on day 41 of the pregnancy. Other religions date it differently.

4. **When 'viability' is reached.** This simply means the time when a baby could survive outside the body of its mother. Although medical science can keep very tiny babies alive, it is still unusual for this to be possible before about 23 weeks of pregnancy. Even then, a premature baby will need very careful nursing.

5. **At birth.** At this moment a baby lives outside its mother and some people feel this is when life begins.

Some people argue that it is not possible to identify the moment when human life begins. They say that life starts at conception, but it is not possible to say when a baby becomes a unique human being because there is continual growth and change. A fertilised egg may later split and become twins, showing that fertilisation is not the start of a human life.

An important question

Although no one can be sure when human life begins, much depends on the answer. Most abortions, for example, are carried out before the sixteenth week of pregnancy, but is the foetus being destroyed a real human being by this time, or not? The question is also important for deciding the morality of scientific experiments on human embryos. Such experiments may be vital in the struggle to discover a cure for some very serious medical conditions. Experiments in the UK are confined to embryos under 14 days old, long before any organ development takes place, but at what stage do embryos become human beings in any meaningful sense? You can see why the question is so important.

The issue, though, is even more complicated than this.

- Hindus, Sikhs and Buddhists believe in reincarnation. They teach that the human soul is eternal and so exists before birth, since it is reborn from a previous existence.
- Christians, Muslims and Jews believe that each individual and unique human being is brought into existence by God at conception or at birth.

All religions are very unhappy about any interference with the reproductive process.

> ✓ **Exam tip**
> This section is a good example of a social/scientific topic that has clear religious implications. REMEMBER – this is an RE exam and the religious implications of a topic are very important. At the same time, you must have an understanding of the social and scientific issues as well.

IMPORTANT WORDS	
Miscarriage;	the spontaneous expulsion of a fertilised embryo or foetus from the womb
Reincarnation;	belief that the soul passes into another body after death

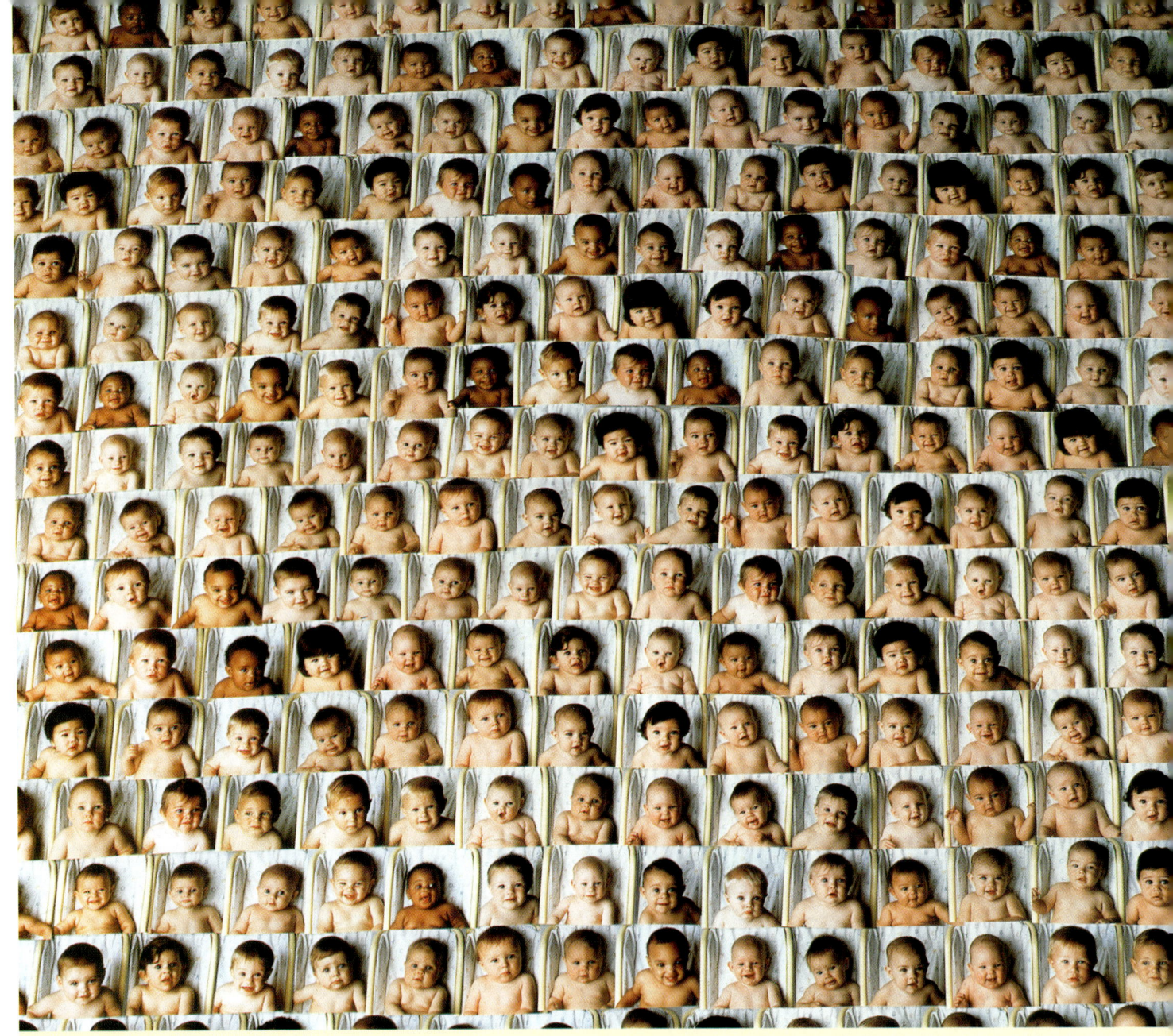

▲ The question of deciding when these young lives began has very important moral and religious implications.

Tasks

1. Describe the process by which a fertilised egg moves from the zygote to the foetus stage.
2. a. Outline the **FIVE** different stages at which it has been suggested that human life begins.
   b. Do any of these stages suggest to you that life begins at that point, rather than any other?
3. Why is it an important matter to decide when life begins?
4. Give **ONE** argument against each of the different views on when life is thought to begin.

SUMMARY

1 During the 9 months of pregnancy an unborn baby moves through many different stages of development.

2 The actual moment at which 'human life' begins is difficult to determine – whether at conception, at the blastocyst stage, when the embryo becomes a soul, at viability or birth.

3 Moral and religious questions relating to certain modern practices, such as abortion, can depend on deciding when life begins.

MATTERS OF LIFE

2:2 The sanctity of life

What do religious people mean when they speak of the 'sanctity of life' and why is it such an important religious belief?

> *God created man in His image, in the image of God He created them; male and female He created them.*
>
> ... THE TANAKH (GENESIS 1.27)

> *I look upon all creatures equally; none are less dear to me and none more dear.*
>
> ... THE BHAGAVAD GITA (9.29)

> *We need to affirm the sacredness of all human life. Every person is somebody because he is a child of God.*
>
> ... MARTIN LUTHER KING, AMERICAN CHRISTIAN LEADER

Religious people often say that they believe in the 'sanctity of life'. By this they mean that there is something holy and sacred about life because it has been created by God, the Supreme Spirit. Judaism, Christianity and Islam believe that this applies just to human life, but Hinduism teaches that it is true of all forms of life.

What does a belief in the sanctity of life mean?

1. **God is the source of all life.** Life begins and ends with God. The creation story, which Jews and Christians share in the book of Genesis, teaches that human beings are made in God's image. This means that human beings have a spiritual dimension, a soul or spirit, which other forms of life do not have. It is this that is capable of loving and worshipping God. In Jewish and Christian teaching it is this dimension that marks human life out as different from animal life.

2. **Life is sacred and so must be preserved.** The strict Jewish laws about keeping the Sabbath day as a day of complete rest are a good example. This was intended to make sure that humans have adequate rest and relaxation in a life of hard work and toil. Yet even these laws, one of God's greatest gifts to the Jewish people, can be broken if a human life is in danger. Nothing is more important than life itself – not even God's laws.

3. **Every life has a purpose.** Each baby has a God-given purpose for its life ahead. Even if someone is born with a serious physical or mental handicap, their life has real purpose and meaning. All human life matters and is important to God. No life should be ended prematurely or wasted.

4. **God alone should decide when each human life ends.** No human being has the right to end their own life. Most religions react to suicide with horror: it is self-murder. No human being has the right to end someone else's life either. This has relevance when the subject of euthanasia is under discussion.

Difficult issues

These ideas are simple and powerful. The problems arise when they are applied to modern issues. Here is a sample of the questions that are raised by them:

1. If God decides when each new life is going to begin, can it ever be right to prevent conception by using contraception?

2. Do doctors have the moral obligation to save life at all costs and in every situation? A person can be 'brain-dead' and yet have their body kept alive by artificial means – is that person alive or dead?

3. Can euthanasia (mercy-killing) ever be justified? Do human beings have the right to decide when their own lives should end or does that right belong to God alone? Does religion condemn suicide and, if so, why?

We shall return to these questions in the pages that follow.

> ✓ **Exam tip**
> When you are giving more than one example to illustrate a point, make sure that they are really different. Do not try to fool the examiner; it will not work!

▲ Everyone, religious or otherwise, agrees that there is something very precious about human life.

Tasks

1. If you believe in the 'sanctity of life', what implications does this have for your belief in God and the value of life?
2. All religious people believe that human beings have a spiritual side – their soul or spirit.
   a. Do you agree that there is a spiritual side to everyone's personality?
   b. If so, how does this spiritual side make itself known? How are you aware of it in your own life?

! Think about …

Most religions teach that there is an essential difference between human and animal life. Do you agree?

IMPORTANT WORDS

Contraception; the deliberate use of methods to prevent pregnancy

Euthanasia; (mercy-killing), the ending of a terminally ill person's life prematurely

SUMMARY

1 All religions believe that life is sacred, created by God.

2 All religions believe that God is the source of all life and life must be preserved; each life has a purpose and God alone has the authority to bring it to a close.

MATTERS OF LIFE

2:3 Fertility and infertility

What can be done today to help couples who are unable to conceive a baby?

Difficulties in conceiving a baby affect far more couples than is generally known. Over 10 per cent of couples have problems starting a family, 1 in every 10 of these, is described as 'inexplicably infertile'. This simply means that, left to their own efforts, they would not become parents. Some of them turn to medical science to help them overcome their problem. However, this kind of help is not readily available from the National Health Service and it costs over £3 000 for a course of treatment.

Ways of assisting conception

In vitro fertilisation. 'In vitro' means 'in glass' and people often refer to this method of conceiving as 'test-tube babies'. This technique was developed to help women with blocked fallopian tubes to conceive, since their eggs could not reach their uterus to be available for fertilisation by their partner's sperm. To solve the problem, a woman is given drugs to help her to produce eggs, which are then collected and fertilised by her partner's sperm outside her body. If the treatment works, embryos are formed and then carefully placed inside the woman's uterus where they can continue to develop until the baby is born. Usually two or three fertilised eggs are replaced to increase the chance of one growing into a baby.

Artificial insemination by donor (AID). AID has been practised in Britain since the 1950s. It is particularly useful when the husband is infertile. Sperm from an anonymous donor are introduced into the neck of the womb from where they travel to the woman's egg. This technique is widely used with animals, but it is still controversial with humans. The child doesn't know who their father is and there is no way that his identity can be discovered. The husband or partner of the woman is the child's legal father. The Roman Catholic Church is strongly opposed to AID considering it to be little different from adultery. Similar objections are raised by other religions.

Artificial insemination by husband (AIH). This takes place when there is a medical reason why a man and a woman cannot conceive – but there is nothing wrong with their eggs or sperm. The husband's sperm are collected and placed in the woman's body to give her the best opportunity of conceiving a baby. Most religious people find this acceptable because it doesn't involve the use of a donor's sperm. The resulting baby is very much the product of husband and wife – with a little helping hand from science!

Egg or sperm storing. It is now possible to store a woman's eggs or a man's sperm in case they are needed at some future time. The man or the woman may die or become infertile in which case the eggs or sperm can be used. A problem is that the eggs can only be stored for a limited time before it becomes dangerous to use them. If a partner dies it must be clear that they would have consented to their eggs or sperm being used.

In 2002, Diane Blood announced that she was expecting her second baby after again using the sperm of her dead husband. Before her first child was conceived she had to go to court to prove that her dead husband would have agreed to his sperm being used.

Fertility drugs. Recent years have seen great steps forward in the development of fertility drugs. A problem is that the number of babies conceived after fertility treatment cannot be controlled. As a result, fertility treatment is likely to result in multiple births.

> **IT'S A FACT**
>
> The first test-tube baby, conceived by in vitro fertilisation, was born in 1978. The procedure is now quite common. In fact, 12 out of every 1000 babies in the UK are conceived in this way.

Surrogacy

Surrogacy takes place when a woman becomes pregnant for someone else who is infertile. This can be done by using the sperm of the infertile woman's husband or using a donor's sperm. For some couples this is the only alternative to childlessness. The Surrogacy Arrangements Act 1985 made it illegal for anyone to advertise surrogacy arrangements or for anyone to pay an agency to make a surrogacy arrangement. It later became illegal for any money, apart from expenses, to be paid for such an agreement.

THE HUMAN FERTILISATION AND EMBRYOLOGY ACT 1990

This important Act states that:

- A man who donates sperm and a woman who donates eggs must remain anonymous.
- A donor, male or female, has no rights over any baby that may result.
- Frozen embryos may be stored for up to 10 years.
- Scientific experiments may be carried out on an embryo for 14 days after conception. After this time it must not be kept alive.

▲ Some people say that it does not matter how children are conceived, as long as they are loved and wanted. Others disagree.

Some parents feel that their son or daughter should know the truth about their conception. However, there could be a negative effect on a child from knowing they were conceived in an unusual way. This could be a real problem if the child was conceived by AID and has no way of knowing their father's identity. In some cases surrogacy becomes a problem when the surrogate mother is not prepared to let a baby go.

Tasks

1. What is infertility?

2. Write **TWO** sentences about each of the following:

    a. IVF   b. AID   c. AIH
    d. egg or sperm storing   e. fertility drugs.

3. a. If you needed to, would you be prepared to use the methods of conception that are mentioned in this unit?

    b. Are there any methods that you think you might feel unhappy about? Give **TWO** reasons for your answer.

4. 'Couples who cannot have a baby should simply accept it and get on with their lives.' How far do you agree with this comment? Give reasons for your answer showing that you have thought about more than one point of view. Refer to religious teachings in your answer.

! Think about ...

In the past, childlessness was looked on as the will or punishment of God. How are things different today?

IMPORTANT WORDS

Infertility; a man or a woman is infertile if they are unable to conceive a baby

Surrogacy; a surrogate mother is one who agrees to carry and give birth to a baby for someone else

SUMMARY

1 A large number of couples are unable to have children – or find it very difficult to do so.

2 There are several ways in which infertile couples can be helped to conceive – including IVF, AIH, AID and other fertility treatments. Many people have reservations about AID.

3 Surrogacy is occasionally used with a woman carrying a baby and giving birth to a baby for someone else, because the child's genetic mother is unable to do so.

MATTERS OF LIFE

2:4 Genetic engineering

What is genetic engineering?

Human genetics and cloning are areas of science that raise very large moral and religious issues. Recent advances in both could allow scientists to cure major medical conditions and also eliminate genetic disorders, such as cystic fibrosis. These advances also raise the possibility of 'designer babies' and the selective breeding of human beings.

Mendel and his peas

Gregor Mendel (1822–84), experimented with peas to see how characteristics were passed on from one generation to another. The study of this process is called 'genetics'. In the nineteenth century he wrote the first four rules of genetics.

1. All organisms get their characteristics from their genes.
2. A pair of genes, one from each parent, controls particular characteristics.
3. Genes may be dominant or recessive.
4. Dominant genes determine characteristics over recessive genes.

In 1953, one of the greatest scientific discoveries of the twentieth century was made by James Watson and Francis Crick. They unravelled DNA – a complex molecule found in all cells – which holds the blueprint for everything that happens in the human body. It has been called the 'building-block of life'. The Human Genome Project, which began in 1990, is an attempt to map out the DNA structure of human beings. This will make it possible to see how individual genes work – and ultimately could lead to the development of drugs to deal with many human diseases.

Manipulating the genes

Within a decade or so it will be possible to manipulate most of the genes in the human body. There are three possible uses of this.

1. **Genetic engineering.** This is the process of manipulating DNA directly, so allowing a particular characteristic to be deleted, altered or replaced. By changing the genetic code the new characteristic will be passed on to the next generation.
2. **Gene therapy.** This involves replacing a defective gene with a new one. This could be done to help people with cystic fibrosis and other conditions.
3. **Xenotransplantation.** This is a method of transplanting organs between one species and another. Pig organs have been used as short-term replacements for human organs in the last few years.

Moral and religious issues

Genetic engineering raises immense moral and religious issues.

- Should insurance companies be allowed to ask for genetic tests before providing life insurance? The results of these tests would tell them a lot about the future life of each person.
- Should unborn foetuses be tested for conditions that lead to an early death? This would then give the parents the opportunity to seek an abortion if they wanted to. It would be possible to tell if a foetus had cystic fibrosis. It would show whether the foetus might have a tendency to contract such a condition as breast cancer later in life.

The questions raised by genetic engineering are very serious and far-reaching. On the positive side some killer diseases could become things of the past by the end of the second decade of the twenty-first century. On the negative side it could mean that the whole map of a person's life was laid bare. It will mean that human beings will be given the opportunity of 'playing God' more and more in the future. This is bound to have a great effect on the faith that many people have in God.

> ✓ **Exam tip**
> Subjects like genetic engineering and cloning are immensely important topics in the modern world. You will not be expected to have a detailed knowledge of them. You will be expected, however, to have a basic understanding and an awareness of the difficult issues that each topic raises.

> **Tasks**
> 1. a. What is genetic engineering?
>   b. Write about DNA and the Human Genome Project.
> 2. Describe **TWO** possible reasons scientists might manipulate the genes in the human body.
> 3. Why are many people very concerned about the possibilities that have been opened by advances in genetic understanding?
> 4. 'Insurance companies should not be allowed to ask for genetic tests. People should be allowed to keep this information secret.' Present **TWO** reasons for this argument and **TWO** against.

▲ Generations of the same family. Children carry a genetic similarity to their parents and grandparents.

IT'S A FACT

The Human Genome Project has involved scientists on many continents, will take 13 years to complete and will cost $3 billion. Even then it will not be able to tell us what each human gene does! For that information we will have to wait a while longer.

IMPORTANT WORDS

Cloning;	producing organisms with identical genetic make-ups
Gene;	one of the units of DNA responsible for passing on special characteristics from parents to offspring
Genetic engineering;	modifying certain genes to control hereditary defects

SUMMARY

1 The key to every aspect of a person's life is to be found in their genes. Genetic engineering involves the manipulation of these genes.

2 Human DNA holds the key to every human being. Once it is fully understood it will be possible to cure many diseases.

3 Genetic engineering, gene therapy and xenotransplantation offer considerable possible future benefits for the human race. They also raise very complicated moral and religious issues.

MATTERS OF LIFE

2:5 Cloning

What is cloning and what moral and religious issues does it raise?

A clone is an individual organism or group of organisms produced from a body cell of its parent and that is genetically identical to it. Everyone seems to have something to say about cloning. It is one of the most controversial medical issues of the day. In this spread, we will discover just what cloning is and some of the fears and concerns that are being expressed about it.

What is cloning?

Cloning is a procedure used to isolate a gene, or a set of genes, before implanting them into an organism. The organism will then duplicate the material. In this way, genetically identical offspring can be produced. Cloning of plants has taken place for a long time. In 1997 the first mammal was cloned. Dolly the sheep opened up a whole new area of debate about cloning, as scientists had performed 'embryo cloning'. People began to ask: 'If a sheep can be cloned, then why not a human being?' and they began to worry. The scientific world was disappointed to learn in 2001 that Dolly had developed arthritis and that this is possibly because she is a clone.

Human cloning will not necessarily lead to the development of identical humans. This is a fear but most of the scientific interest is in 'therapeutic cloning' and not in duplicating human beings. Therapeutic cloning is the creation of human embryos in a laboratory to extract embryonic stem cells from them. These stem cells can develop into any cells in the human body. The genetic material that they provide could then be implanted back into a person's body. It could be used to cure heart problems or to produce entire organs for transplants. The body would not reject the transplant as the DNA would be an exact match. A leukaemia patient, for example, could have the perfect match for a bone marrow transplant produced by cloning. The possibilities are almost endless and, in the eyes of many people, almost wholly beneficial. Others, though, are not so sure.

Arguments for therapeutic cloning

- It could eliminate heart disease and heart attacks.
- It could produce human cells to deal with serious burns and brain deterioration, for example.
- It could reduce infertility.
- It brings in the possibility of reversing the ageing process.

> *The suffering that can be relieved is staggering. This new technology heralds a new era of unparalleled advancement in medicine if people will release their fears and let the benefits begin. Why should another child die from leukaemia when, if the technology is allowed, we should be able to cure it in a few years' time?*
>
> **... HUMAN CLONING FOUNDATION**

Arguments against therapeutic cloning

- It is immoral because it suggests that some human characteristics are more important than others.
- Cloning could allow people to choose their perfect baby – 'designer babies'.
- Scientists will eventually be able to clone entire human beings.
- Cloning destroys the individual nature of human life – with all its imperfections.
- Cloning would be against God's will.

So, what is the future for human cloning? There are many benefits to be gained from the process, but are the moral and religious objections too important to be simply swept to one side? Will the human race end up as replicas and clones? What other problems could be caused if many killer diseases were curable and life were prolonged noticeably? These questions go to the heart of what we believe about life.

> ✓ **Exam tip**
> Cloning is a subject that is worth following in newspapers and on television. New technologies and developments are taking place all the time. Keep up to date on this and other topics in the news.

▲ The cloning of Dolly the sheep made people realise that the cloning of humans may soon be possible. However, scientists produced many disfigured animals before managing to create Dolly.

Tasks

1.a. What is therapeutic cloning?

  b. Describe **TWO** possible uses to which therapeutic cloning might be put.

  c. Would you enjoy living at a time when therapeutic cloning was a normal part of life? Give **TWO** reasons for your answer.

  d. Why do you think that human cloning, in any form, is highly controversial? Why are so many people worried about it?

2. Give **THREE** reasons to support research into human cloning and **THREE** reasons why people are very doubtful about it.

3. 'All human cloning should be banned.' Do you agree with this comment? Give reasons for your answer showing that you have thought about more than one point of view. Refer to religious teachings in your answer.

IMPORTANT WORDS

Embryo cloning; removing cells from an embryo to grow into a separate embryo – the method used to create Dolly the sheep

Therapeutic cloning; cloning parts of the body that can then be used to cure specific diseases and illnesses

SUMMARY

1 Cloning isolates a gene before implanting it in an organism, which then duplicates it. Cloning has been successful in plants and animals.

2 Therapeutic cloning would allow stem cells to provide genetic material that could then be implanted back into a person. This would offer a cure for many illnesses.

3 There are strong arguments for and against cloning.

MATTERS OF LIFE

2:6 Organ transplants and blood transfusions

What moral and religious issues are thrown up by organ transplantation?

> **IT'S A FACT**
>
> It is now possible to transplant at least 25 different organs and tissues – including kidney, pancreas, heart, lung, cornea and liver – from one person to another. These operations were revolutionary when first introduced, but are now routine.

In the last 20 years it has become possible to transplant many different organs and tissues. New techniques are being introduced all the time to do this and the range of transplants now available offer thousands of people the chance of a greatly improved lifestyle. At the same time these techniques have introduced a series of hotly debated issues ranging from our attitudes to the dead body, the scarcity of available organs and the use of animal organs and tissues in the future. At the moment, many more people need organ transplants than there are organs available and it is a lottery whether one is available when needed. For the system to be widely available more people need to donate their own organs or those of a loved one who has died.

Blood transfusions

Blood transfusions have become part of the routine of modern medicine. In the UK, blood is donated freely and countless lives are saved as a result. This is now completely safe for the person giving and the person receiving blood because very stringent screening processes are in place. The Jehovah's Witnesses, a small Christian group, are well known for their opposition to blood transfusions – but they are alone amongst religious groups in having this opinion. Their refusal stems back to a time when passages in the Bible, instructing followers not to 'eat' blood, were taken to include transfusions. Adult members of the group may refuse to have a transfusion and put their own life in danger. Occasionally a court is involved if a parent refuses permission for a child to have a life-saving transfusion. Usually, in this situation, the court overrules the religious beliefs of the parents to save the child.

Organ transplantation

Two kinds of human organ transplantation can take place.

1. **Transplants in which the donor is living.** Other than bone marrow transplants, this is usually only done in the case of kidney failure. There must be a perfect match between donor and recipient for this to be possible. The person who gives a kidney can manage quite normally on just one kidney as long as that kidney remains healthy. In 1989, it became illegal for someone to be paid to donate a kidney in the UK, although this still happens in some Third World countries, like India, where comparatively large sums of money are paid to donors.

2. **Transplants in which the donor has just died.** This may take place after someone dies in a car accident. Many people carry donor cards giving permission for their organs to be taken. In some cases immediate relatives give their permission. For the organ to be useful, however, transplantation must take place very soon after death and this makes it a very difficult, emotional experience for surviving relatives to come to terms with.

Arguments for organ transplantation

- There is no risk to dead donors.
- The death of someone can give new life to someone else.
- It is a 'last-chance' solution for many people. If they do not have a transplant they will die.
- The donor makes a contribution to society because the recipient has the chance of a new life.

Arguments against organ transplantation

- It is sometimes difficult to define death. Many people are against taking organs from brain-dead patients.
- If the donor is living there is some risk involved.
- It is sometimes difficult, or very upsetting, to obtain permission for an organ to be used from relatives soon after death.
- What is meant by giving 'free consent' to having one's organs used?
- Transplant operations are very expensive and take resources away from other, equally needy, medical cases.

As we shall see, the main religions have little difficulty with the moral and religious issues thrown up by transplant surgery, although some doubt was expressed when the procedure was in its infancy.

Muslims may experience a dilemma as the body is seen as the possession of Allah both before and after death. Although this is a position that has changed in recent years, as society has grown more used to organ transplantations taking place. For Christians, Jews and Sikhs organ transplantation raises few religious problems.

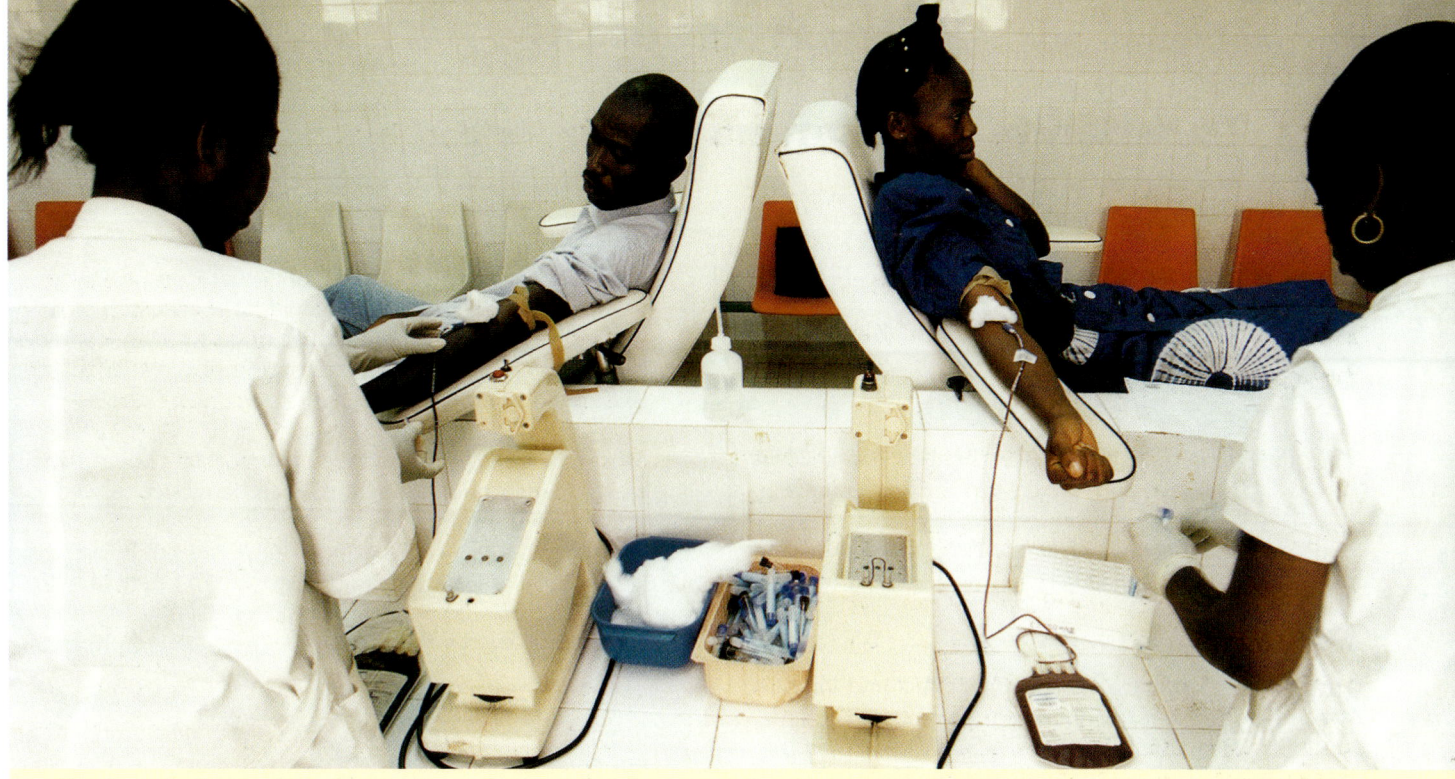

▲ Blood transfusions and organ transplants raise few moral or religious objections. Although Jehovah's Witnesses were against both, they now allow organ transplants.

> *If one is in a position to donate an organ to save another's life, it is obligatory to do so, even if the donor never knows who the beneficiary will be. The basic principle of Jewish ethics – 'the infinite worth of the human being' – also includes donations of corneas, since eyesight restoration is considered a life-saving operation.*
>
> **... DR MOSES TENDTLER**

Tasks

1. What are the **TWO** different kinds of organ transplantation?
2. a. What are the main reasons someone might be opposed to the idea of organ transplantation?
   b. What arguments might someone put forward for allowing organ transplants to take place?

IMPORTANT WORDS

Jehovah's Witnesses; a small Protestant group formed in the nineteenth century – they are opposed to blood transfusions

! Think about ...

In 2001, after a two-year enquiry, it emerged that Alder Hey Children's Hospital in Liverpool had stockpiled the organs of 3500 children. These organs were removed without parental knowledge or consent. Use the internet to research issues relating to the retention of body parts for medical research.

SUMMARY

1 Apart from Jehovah's Witnesses, most people are perfectly happy with the idea of blood transfusions.

2 Organ donations can be taken from living or dead donors. The arguments about organ transplantation are different depending on the nature of the donation.

3 The only one of the six main religions that had found difficulty in the past with organ donation has been Islam, although the attitude of this religion has changed in recent years.

MATTERS OF LIFE

2:7 Christianity and matters of life

What does Christianity teach about infertility and medical research?

Like other religions, Christianity teaches that human life is sacred and human beings are created to have a unique spiritual relationship with God. It is within this understanding that we look at infertility, genetic research, cloning and transplant surgery.

Infertility

There is no specific teaching in the Bible about infertility because no form of treatment was possible at the time the Bible was written. If people were childless then this was because God had intended it to be that way. The following quote demonstrates how the Old Testament described the childlessness of one woman.

> *Hannah had no children ... because the Lord had kept her from having children.*
>
> ... **THE BIBLE (1 SAMUEL 1.2,5)**

Now, of course, the medical situation is very different. The general Christian attitude, expressed by most Churches, is that infertility treatment is acceptable as long as it is the wife's egg and the husband's sperm that are used (IVF and AIH). There is discontent, though, with AID, since this involves a third party and so bears a moral similarity to adultery. The Roman Catholic Church is opposed to all forms of fertility treatment since they involve 'unnatural' sexual acts. To obtain the man's sperm, for instance, masturbation is involved and this is a sin.

> *Techniques that entail the dissociation of husband and wife, by the intrusion of a person other than the couple ... are gravely immoral.*
>
> ... **CATECHISM OF THE CATHOLIC CHURCH, 1994**

Genetic engineering and cloning

Christians believe that human beings have a God-given responsibility to look after the whole of creation. Some are worried that scientists may, through genetic engineering, overstep the authority that God has given them. Others believe that the work of science can greatly enhance the quality of human life and so it is welcomed. Most Churches accept genetic engineering, if it is going to be used to cure disease.

Most Christians feel distinctly uncomfortable about the idea of cloning human beings. Each baby is conceived, they believe, through the co-operation of a man, a woman and God. This unique 'trinity' was put in place by God at creation and it would be wrong to interfere with it. It would also be wrong to clone a person just to obtain spare parts, even if these could be used to cure disease.

Although science can bring many long-term benefits to the human race, we allow it to step over its boundaries at our peril. Some Christians have pointed out the possible benefits to the human race if therapuetic cloning were allowed to develop along very carefully controlled lines.

Embryology and transplant surgery

The Roman Catholic Church is strongly opposed to all embryo research. It believes that life begins at conception and any experimentation on embryos is wrong. Other Churches, though, do not object to such experimentation as long as the research is properly controlled. The Church of England supports research on embryos up to 14 days old – as the present UK law allows. Most Churches also support the donation of organs; seeing this as the gift of life from one person to another. Blood transfusions are accepted by all Christian groups, except Jehovah's Witnesses, without any difficulty.

> *Jesus of Nazareth was a healer. He cured diseases and showed that God's purposes include overcoming 'those things in His creation that spoil it and that diminish the life of his children'. Clearly, where genetic manipulation is the means of healing diseases – in animals or humans – it is to be welcomed.*
>
> ... **METHODIST CHURCH, 'WHAT THE CHURCHES SAY'**

▲ The gift of new life is treated within the Christian community with great excitement.

> ✓ **Exam tip**
> REMEMBER – it is important not to waffle in your answer. You can only be given marks for the facts that you present to the examiner.

Tasks

1. Summarise, briefly, Christian teaching about:
   a. infertility   b. embryo research
   c. blood transfusions   d. genetic engineering
   e. cloning.
2. Take **TWO** of these issues and summarise your own attitude towards them.

IMPORTANT WORDS

Church of England; the most important Church in England, part of the worldwide Anglican Church

> ❗ **Think about ...**
> Do you think that every couple has the 'right' to become parents? Explain your answer.

SUMMARY

1 Whilst the Roman Catholic Church is opposed to infertility treatment, other Churches find it acceptable in most situations.

2 The Roman Catholic Church is opposed to all embryo research, but all Churches accept that organ transplantation is a good thing.

3 Most Churches accept that genetic engineering may be good if it helps to cure disease, but great reservations are expressed about human cloning.

4 Therapuetic cloning receives general support from the Church and individual Christians. They believe it holds out great hope for curing fatal diseases.

MATTERS OF LIFE

2:8 Judaism and Islam, and matters of life

What do Judaism and Islam teach about infertility and medical research?

Both Judaism and Islam believe in the God who is the creator of all life. Children are seen as a very important part of family and social life. Both religions consider children to be gifts from God.

JUDAISM

> *Whoever destroys a single life is considered as if he had destroyed the whole world, and whoever saves a single life as if he had saved the world.*
>
> ... THE MISHNAH, A JEWISH HOLY BOOK

Infertility. IVF and AIH treatment for infertility do not cause any problems for Jews. Many rabbis have taught that if procreation cannot take place through normal sexual intercourse then other means are acceptable. Family life is extremely important within the Jewish community and infertility is a source of great sadness. Many Jews feel unhappy about AID as it can be seen to be a form of adultery and they are also concerned about the status of the child. Other Jews, though, accept AID. They argue that, even if the donor remains the biological father in Jewish law, no sin has been committed and the child is still fully legitimate. Surrogacy is forbidden by most rabbinic authorities. One reason being that a child's religious identity comes through its Jewish mother.

Genetic engineering and cloning. Genetic research is supported by most Jews, because the Tanakh clearly teaches that everything should be done to eliminate disease. Some, though, disagree with research on embryos since an embryo is a human life and killing is forbidden. There is, as yet, no clear teaching by the Jewish community on cloning. The Torah teaches that it is right to use any means to save human life and cloning to produce body parts and tissue may be covered by this. Judaism, as other religions, would certainly be against cloning human beings since that would be to challenge the authority of God, the Creator.

Transplant surgery. Most Jews are happy to allow transplant surgery as long as the organ is taken from a living person, but many are unhappy with the idea of an organ being taken from someone who has died.

ISLAM

> *He bestows (children) male or female according to His will (and plan).*
>
> ... THE QUR'AN (42.49)

Infertility. The procreation of children is a very important part of a Muslim marriage. Life can be difficult for a couple who cannot have children. Muslims recognise that if a couple has problems conceiving a baby they may need medical help. There is no objection to IVF or AIH, but Muslims see little difference between AID and adultery, which is strictly forbidden in the Qur'an. Surrogacy is also forbidden because, as the Qur'an teaches, no one can be a child's mother, except the woman who carried it. Muslim men are allowed by the Qur'an to have up to four wives and this may happen if one wife is unable to give her husband children – so making surrogacy unnecessary.

Genetic engineering and cloning. Muslims are divided over genetic engineering. Some maintain that Allah alone can determine the genetic make-up of each man and woman and any attempt to alter this is forbidden. Certainly, any attempt to create life is against the will of Allah. The cloning of plants and animals does not cause any problems, but there are great doubts over the wisdom of cloning humans. Some Muslims, though, do accept that cloning might be acceptable and necessary if it leads to cures for life-threatening illnesses.

> *If anyone has saved a life, it would be as if he has saved the life of the whole people.*
>
> ... THE QUR'AN (5.32)

Embryology and transplant surgery. The Qur'an teaches that all human life is sacred. Embryos left over from IVF treatment may be used for medical research, but they cannot be created specifically for this purpose. Any organs used in transplantation must be given freely. Blood transfusions can be used where necessary.

Tasks

1. Write down **THREE** ways in which Jews and Muslims agree in their approach to the different matters of life.
2. Write down **THREE** ways in which Jews and Muslims disagree in their approach to the different matters of life.
3. What is the attitude of both Judaism and Islam to infertility and genetic engineering?
4. Both Judaism and Islam are strongly opposed to adultery. How might this affect the attitude of the two religions to some forms of fertility treatment?

SUMMARY

❶ Jews and Muslims are willing to use IVF and AIH; both are opposed to AID. Both religions also ban surrogacy.

❷ Jews and Muslims give limited support to genetic engineering and support plant and animal cloning. Many Jews and Muslims see the medical advantages of cloning, although both are opposed to the cloning of human beings.

❸ Jews and Muslims are divided among themselves about the use of organs taken from dead people for transplant surgery.

▼ The Jewish faith recognises that it is not always easy to reconcile traditional faith and modern issues such as genetic engineering and cloning.

MATTERS OF LIFE

2:9 Hinduism, Sikhism and Buddhism, and matters of life

What is the teaching of Hinduism, Sikhism and Buddhism on infertility and medical research?

Each of these three religions believes in reincarnation, which means that each soul has many existences on earth. Human life is very precious, but it is not the only opportunity that a person has. Inevitably, this must colour each religion's attitude to infertility, genetic engineering and cloning.

■ HINDUISM

> *The one who rules over both knowledge and ignorance ... alone presides over womb after womb and thus over all visible forms and all the sources of birth.*
>
> ... SVETASVATARA UPANISHAD (5.2)

Infertility. Being able to have children is very important to Hindus and they are happy to seek medical advice if there is a problem. IVF and AIH do not present a problem, but Hindus would not use AID as children would not know what caste they belonged to.

Genetic engineering and cloning. All Hindus are working their way towards moksha – spiritual liberation from the body. This is the aim and goal of their human existence. Cloning has to be seen in the light of this as it does not help the Hindu in their quest to reach this place of freedom from all earthly restraints. Cloning may be acceptable, however, if its intention is to relieve human suffering.

Embryology and organ transplants. Hindus could not accept any scientific experiment in which embryos were destroyed. As the relief of suffering is important to Hindus, so organ transplantation does not present a problem. Blood transfusions are also acceptable.

■ SIKHISM

> *By Divine Law are beings created .... Others by His Law are whistled around in cycles of births and deaths.*
>
> ... ADI GRANTH (JAPJI 2)

Infertility. The impetus to have children is strong in the Sikh tradition. Male children are important to continue the family name and to look after parents when they reach old age. If natural methods of achieving conception fail, then AIH and IVF are permitted. AID and surrogacy are not allowed because these are seen as unnatural.

Genetic engineering and cloning. Sikh teaching does not rule out gene therapy, but unease is expressed about cloning. It is recognised that traditional teaching based on the holy book does not cover such modern issues. It does, though, seem to offer considerable benefits to the human race and so should not be ruled out by Sikh teaching.

Embryology and organ transplants. Sikhs believe that an embryo is a human being from the moment of conception. The production of embryos just for scientific experimentation is not acceptable. Both blood transfusions and organ transplants are permitted. Organs taken from living or dead people can be used to save life.

■ BUDDHISM

> *Whoever, O monks, would nurse me, he should nurse the sick.*
>
> ... THE BUDDHA

Infertility. There is little pressure on Buddhists to marry and have children. Many of them spend time as monks or nuns. There is no clear Buddhist teaching on infertility treatment.

Genetic engineering and cloning. Buddhists are very worried about the implications of genetic engineering. They are against any experiments that involve cruelty to animals and plants. For Buddhists, the end, such as a cure for serious diseases, does not justify the means if that involves acts of cruelty to the non-human world.

Embryology and organ transplants. The Buddhist emphasis is very much on the relief of the sick. Buddhists believe that it is wrong to kill any living thing, but disagree over whether an embryo is a human being. Buddhists are left free to make up their own minds about organ transplantation and blood transfusions.

> ! **Think about ...**
>
> Buddhists do not believe that the end, such as a cure for cancer, justifies the means if this involves acts of cruelty to the non-human world.
> Do you agree with them? Give **TWO** reasons for your answer.

Tasks

1. What do each of the three religions believe about embryology and organ transplants?
2. What do each of the three religions believe about genetic engineering and cloning?
3. Why are Hindus and Sikhs happy to seek help if they are having problems starting a family?

IMPORTANT WORD

Moksha; term used in Hinduism for liberation from the cycle of rebirth, which is the goal of all human existence

SUMMARY

1 Hinduism is happy with most medical procedures as long as they relieve human suffering. AID, though, is not acceptable.

2 Sikhs are unhappy with AID, but other forms of fertility treatment and organ transplants are acceptable.

3 Any scientific procedure that involves cruelty to animals is unacceptable to Buddhists. The relief of human suffering is a strong consideration.

▼ Buddhist children being taught. Like other religions, Buddhism is slowly working out its attitude to modern issues.

MATTERS OF LIFE

✓ Exam help ...

In this section you have studied some very important topics that go to the very heart of what people believe about life. Religious people disagree over just when life begins but they agree on the sacredness and sanctity of human life. Much can be done today to help couples who cannot conceive but we are only beginning to understand the genetic structure of each human being. Therapeutic cloning may be acceptable to the majority but human cloning is not. Many people find the use of dead bodies for organ donation problematic.

1. What is meant by in vitro fertilisation and which people can it help?

1. About 10 per cent of all couples have trouble with conceiving and many turn to IVF. One of the most common problems is that the woman's egg does not reach the uterus/IVF ('in glass') brings together the egg and the sperm in a laboratory. Fertilisation takes place in a test-tube – hence 'test-tube babies'/embryos are formed and placed back in the woman's body (more than one) and the pregnancy develops as normal.

2.a. What is cloning?
b. What is the attitude of the world religions to cloning?

2.a. Cloning involves isolating a gene before placing it in an organism/the organism will then duplicate itself/has been carried out on plants for a long time/recently on an animal (Dolly the sheep)/most scientific interest is in therapeutic cloning/stem cells are taken from embryos/can be used to cure genetic abnormalities in humans.

b. **Christianity:** very unhappy about human cloning/each person is a special creation of God/also unhappy about therapeutic cloning – some Christians accept therapeutic cloning as long as it is carefully controlled.

Judaism: no clear teaching/Torah teaches that almost anything is permissible if it saves human life/this may include therapeutic cloning though some oppose cloning as it challenges God's authority.

Islam: cloning of plants and animals does not cause a problem/great doubt about cloning humans – may be acceptable if it leads to cures for major diseases.

Hinduism: all Hindus are working towards moksha and cloning does not help this/therapeutic cloning may be acceptable in certain conditions.

Sikhism: God is the creator of all that exists/it is the 'divine spark' in everyone that makes humans unique/Guru Granth Sahib does not offer any guidance/may be acceptable if it leads to cure for diseases.

Buddhism: concern centres around reincarnation/there is no start to life/how would this be affected by cloning?/all creatures are unique, so cloning is unacceptable.

Conclusion – religious concern centres on the God-given individuality of people/cloning destroys this/would seem to challenge the idea of special creation/we cannot be sure of the long-term implications of cloning/selection of desirable characteristics means that so-called 'undesirable' characteristics can be removed –/is this in the long-term interests of the human race?

CHAPTER 3
Matters of death

In this section we will look at some of the most sensitive issues in modern society. We try to determine what responsibility a civilised society has towards the sick, elderly and disabled in its midst. Who should care for them? We debate whether modern medicine should devote itself to keeping a terminally ill patient alive, at all costs. We ask whether life is always better than death – even if the quality of that life is very poor. We consider what kind of support can be given to people who are driven by circumstances to contemplate taking their own life. Not surprisingly, the world religions have a great deal to contribute to the debate about these issues. As you work your way through this section, several questions will come back time and time again.

What is death?

Is a person dead when their heart stops? Is it possible to be brain dead and yet breathing? What about the people who can be kept 'alive' almost indefinitely on a life-support machine? When the machine is switched off, is the person being killed? Is a person in a 'persistent vegetative state' alive or dead?

Is there such a thing as life after death?

The world religions agree that there is, but disagree over the form that it takes. There is a strong disagreement between the religions that believe in the resurrection of the body and those that are committed to reincarnation. Are people re-born many times or resurrected to eternal life after one life on earth? Is there a time of judgement, reward or punishment following death? If there is a judgement to come, on what basis will people be judged?

Does anyone have the right to end their own life or help to end the life of someone else?

Is a person the master of their own fate, as many non-religious people believe – or does the right of deciding just when life should end belong to God alone? If it belongs to God, as the world religions insist, is it possible to accept everything, including suffering, as part of the Divine will?

Who should take the responsibility of caring for those who are old, sick and terminally ill in the community?

Traditionally, the responsibility for this has always fallen on members of the immediate family and this is the teaching of the world religions. Things have changed in the modern world, though, and often it is not practical for a family to carry the whole burden. Who then must share it? The government with social security payments, old peoples' homes and nursing homes? The local community? The faith communities taking responsibility for the needs of their elderly and sick members?

These are some of the issues that will concern us in the following pages. As you study them, you should begin to explore your own attitudes to these fundamental matters. They are certain to become more important in the years ahead.

MATTERS OF DEATH

3:1 The sick and the elderly

What particular problems do old people face in our society – and why?

In the UK more and more people are surviving into old age. Look at the statistics for a moment:

- There are now four times as many people over the age of 65 as there were in 1900. At the moment 17 per cent of the population has reached retirement age – compared with just 6 per cent in India and 3 per cent in Brazil. By the year 2020, the retirement age for men and women in the UK will be equalised at 65.
- BBC news reported, in March 2002, that by 2005 the majority of Africans can expect to die before they reach the age of 48. In contrast, the UK average is 74 years for men and 79 years for women.

These statistics, by themselves, present an enormous problem. The UK now has to support over 10 million retired people. Those who do not work have to be supported by those who do – this is the basic principle of the welfare state. As people live to an older age, so they have to be supported for longer.

Getting old

Following are the main problems associated with growing old.

1. **Failing health.** A person in their 70s is seven times more likely to call on the services of their doctor than someone in their 30s. Over 50 per cent of all doctors' prescriptions are given to those over the age of 65. Diseases like arthritis, rheumatism and bronchitis are much more likely to affect the elderly. Life-threatening illnesses like strokes, heart attacks and cancer become more likely as a person grows older.

2. **Poverty.** Once a person retires they will almost certainly experience a drop in income. Over 70 per cent of senior citizens depend on the Old Age Pension (which amounts to only 15 per cent of the average male earnings) as their sole source of income. The older the person, the poorer they are likely to be – especially single and widowed women.

3. **Loneliness.** Over 2 million old people live on their own. The vast majority of these are women – men tend to be older than their wives and die earlier. Bereavement, being housebound or disabled increases the sense of isolation that so many feel.

Improved standards of health care mean that old people can stay fit and healthy longer. They find they have more time on their hands. Old age can be a time when the family worries and anxieties of the past are largely over. They can take up new hobbies and develop interests. Grandchildren are a great source of pleasure and joy.

> *It ought to be lovely to be old*
> *To be full of the peace that comes of experience*
> *And wrinkled ripe fulfilment.*
>
> **... DH LAWRENCE (PANSIES: POEMS 1929)**

▼ People are living longer and finding new activities to enjoy in their later life.

▲ There are many religious and non-religious clubs, which give elderly people the chance to meet together.

Caring for the elderly

In the past, relatives supported older members of the family. Several generations of the same family lived together or close by. This arrangement is called the 'extended family' and usually still exists within the Asian communities, where it is seen as an honour to look after the elderly relatives.

Now, children often move away from parents to go to university or to work. Most families have just two generations living under the same roof – they are called 'nuclear families'.

Until it becomes impossible, most elderly people prefer to continue living under their own roof. Meals-on-wheels and support from the social services, together with regular visits from family and friends, often make this possible. Alternatively, there is sheltered accommodation. When independence becomes impossible, there are local authority nursing and old people's homes, as well as privately run homes. These are 'means-tested' and people pay as much as they can afford. They may, however, need to sell their homes to pay the bill and this is strongly resented, as this is often the only real 'wealth' that many people have to pass on to their children.

> *Once people are classified as old they tend to be treated as dependent and as physically and mentally incapacitated, irrespective of their characteristics as individuals ... . People who look old frequently state that they do not feel old.*
>
> **... FULCHER AND SCOTT (SOCIOLOGY, OXFORD)**

IMPORTANT WORDS

Nuclear family; modern family arrangement in which parents and children live in the same house, with the rest of the family scattered

Welfare state; situation in the UK where medical and educational facilities are provided free at the point of delivery

Tasks

1. What is **ONE** result of more and more people living well into old age?
2. What are **THREE** of the consequences of growing old?
3. What are **TWO** possible benefits of growing old?
4. 'Everything should be done to help old people remain independent until the last possible moment. How could this be made possible?

SUMMARY

1 Many more people are living into 'old age' now than 100 years ago.

2 Failing health, poverty and loneliness are three of the main problems associated with growing old.

3 Many people are finding increasing enjoyment in the opportunities that old age presents. They may also have several grandchildren.

MATTERS OF DEATH

3:2 The hospice movement

What is a hospice and what is distinctive about the care it offers the terminally ill?

> *By giving terminally ill children permission to be who they are and ensuring that they are in a loving, supportive environment, it is possible to help them to meet death with a dignity and with a nobility which in no way denies grief.*
>
> **... MOTHER FRANCES DOMINICA,**
> **FOUNDER OF HOSPICE FOR CHILDREN IN OXFORD**

In the Middle Ages hospices were small institutions that looked after the elderly, the sick and travellers passing through. They were places of physical and spiritual refreshment. Most of the hospices had a Christian foundation and were run by monks or nuns, since the spiritual care of the sick and dying has long been a major task undertaken by the Church. The modern hospice movement was started at the start of the nineteenth century.

The modern hospice movement

The modern hospice movement began when a group of Irish nuns, the Sisters of Charity, established a home for the dying in Dublin towards the end of the nineteenth century. In 1900, five nuns from the Order arrived in England to set up a home for the terminally ill in the East End of London. Within a few years, St Joseph's Hospice was up and running. Almost 60 years later a young nurse, Cicely Saunders, began her nursing career there but suffered a back injury. In 1967, she set up the St Christopher's Hospice nearby and there are now over 100 in-patient hospices in England offering, at any one time, care and support for 2000 patients who are terminally ill. The first hospice in the USA was opened in 1974 and now about 2000 of them look after the needs of 300 000 patients. In both countries, though, the demand for places far outstrips the number of beds available. As there is no government grant available for the work, hospices depend on fund-raising, personal donations and money left in the wills of well-wishers.

The aims of the hospice movement

Whatever their religious background, all hospices have the same basic objective – to offer care and support to patients, friends and relatives at the most difficult time in their lives. Within this overall objective hospices have three aims.

1. **To relieve pain.** Hospices specialise in pain control. Doctors and nurses working in hospices have led the way in recent years in 'palliative care' – the control of pain.
2. **To help patients, friends and relatives to face up to forthcoming death.** It is very important that people confront their worries and anxieties about dying. Although most hospices have a Christian foundation, no attempt is made to persuade patients to become Christian believers. That would be a betrayal of the trust that patients and relatives place in the staff. Hospices are open to people of all faiths and those of no faith.
3. **To care for the mental and emotional needs of friends and relatives.** Hospices exist to help people before and after their bereavement. This is why hospices believe that counselling is a very important part of their work.

How hospices help

Because places are limited most hospices are only able to offer short-term residential care. To begin with, patients enter for just a week or two. As their health declines they enter for longer, but they can choose to die either in the hospice or in their home. If they wish to die at home, then Macmillan nurses, who specialise in caring for the terminally ill, are able to offer them the help and support they need.

> *Anything which says to the very ill that they are a burden to their family and that they would be better off dead is unacceptable. What sort of society could let its old folk die because 'they are in the way'?*
>
> **... DR CICELY SAUNDERS,**
> **FOUNDER OF ST. CHRISTOPHER'S HOSPICE**

! Think about ...

'Hospices do such important work in looking after those who are dying that their work should be supported financially by the state.' Do you agree with this opinion?

Tasks

1. Why do you think that many people who are not religious support the hospice movement?
2. What is the overall objective of the hospice movement?
3. What are the main aims of the hospice movement?
4. How do hospices help the terminally ill and their families?

SUMMARY

1 The modern hospice movement began at the start of the twentieth century and later developed through the work of Dr Cicely Saunders and others.

2 A hospice helps to alleviate pain (palliative care); helps family, friends and patients face up to death and cares for the needs of those bereaved.

3 Most hospices offer short-term care and long-term help.

▼ Personal relationships are very important as care is offered to the terminally ill.

MATTERS OF DEATH

3:3 Euthanasia – the facts

What is euthanasia?

Is it ever right to end a life medically? Is it the quality of a person's life, rather than its length that really matters? In the following pages, we will look at the arguments for and against euthanasia.

The word 'euthanasia' comes from two Greek words and means a 'good' or 'easy' death. In today's debate, it has come to mean 'mercy killing' and refers to bringing a peaceful, but premature, end to dying. Euthanasia can take different forms.

1. **Involuntary euthanasia.** Involuntary euthanasia happens when a sick person is too ill to make their wishes known and a person believes it is in the patient's best interest. Examples include:
   - not making the effort needed to keep a person alive by resuscitation after a heart-attack
   - not treating complications, like pneumonia, because of a person's frail condition
   - withdrawing an intravenous tube feeding a person judged to be brain-dead or in a PVS (persistent vegetative state). A court case in 1993 allowed doctors to stop treating a person in a long-term coma from which recovery was impossible.

> **IT'S A FACT**
>
> According to the British Social Attitudes Survey (1997) there are, in Britain, at any one time, about 2000 people who have been in a persistent vegetative state for longer than six months. Eventually treatment will be withheld from each of them and they will be allowed to die.

2. **Voluntary euthanasia.** This takes place at the request of the patient, who asks to be allowed to die. This is different from suicide since it enlists the help of a third person – whether a doctor, a relative or a friend – because the person is unable to take their own life. At the moment voluntary euthanasia is illegal in the UK. It has been legal in the Netherlands, with very strict guidelines, since 2000. (In the UK, since the Suicide Act 1961 suicide itself has not been a criminal offence.)

The Voluntary Euthanasia Society, also known as EXIT, has argued since the 1930s that people who are well should be able to make 'living wills', which are witnessed and signed giving permission for their life to be ended by legal means if that life becomes intolerable. It also wants terminally ill people to be able to sign a consent form to have their lives ended. There should be, EXIT argues, a 15-day cooling-off period after signing during which patients can change their mind.

3. **Active euthanasia.** This is when a person deliberately acts to end a life.

4. **Passive euthanasia.** This means 'letting' a person die by withholding treatment. In 1999, Neil Lane from Staffordshire wanted to stop his wife Lorraine, who was in a coma, receiving food and water. It has been argued that this is not the same as euthanasia, which is often about actively giving treatment that would hasten or bring about death.

Those who support the hospice movement argue that it is not necessary for anyone to die in great pain now, since acute pain can be controlled by drugs. They conclude that euthanasia is both unnecessary and socially undesirable. Although most hospices have grown out of the Christian Church's concern for the sick and dying, they are also supported by many humanists who believe that life should be seen through to its natural end. However, there are some Christians who argue that voluntary euthanasia should be made legal in certain strictly controlled situations.

The British Social Attitudes Survey (1997)
People were interviewed to see how many supported voluntary euthanasia. The survey found that:
- 86 per cent thought it should be allowed for those with an incurable illness or on a life-support machine
- 58 per cent thought it should be allowed for those in an irreversible coma
- 51 per cent thought it should be allowed for those who were not in pain but were totally dependent on others.

> **! Think about …**
>
> Look at the survey findings above. For which conditions did more than 50 per cent of those interviewed think that voluntary euthanasia should be allowed? Write down **TWO** comments to show how you feel about these findings. Do you think that they give a true indication of how the majority of people feel about euthanasia? Give **TWO** reasons for your answer.

▲ More than almost any other modern issue, euthanasia raises very strong moral and religious issues. This photo shows Diane and Brian Pretty in court in 2002.

In 2002, 43-year-old Diane Pretty went to court. She was suffering from a degenerative disease of the nervous system, which prevented her from doing anything for herself. She wanted the court to allow her husband to help her to die without himself facing the charge of murder.

Diane took the case to the European Court of Human Rights after the British legal system ruled against her. Once again judges ruled that Diane could not be helped to kill herself. Three days after she lost her right-to-die challenge, Diane started having breathing difficulties. Ten days later, on 11 May 2002, Diane died.

Tasks

1. a. What is euthanasia?
   b. What is the difference between euthanasia and suicide?
   c. Why do you think that suicide has been legal in the UK since the early 1960s, whilst voluntary euthanasia remains illegal?
2. Explain in **ONE** paragraph the difference between involuntary and voluntary euthanasia.

Exam tip
Euthanasia is a highly emotive subject. You will be marked on the evidence you produce to support your arguments – not the strength of your feelings!

IMPORTANT WORDS

Active euthanasia; someone, other than the patient, deliberately ends the patient's life

Passive euthanasia; withholding treatment from incurable patients until they die

SUMMARY

1 There are different forms of euthanasia: involuntary, voluntary, active and passive. Many people would like to see voluntary euthanasia made legal in this country.

2 People who argue for voluntary euthanasia accept that there should be a 'cooling-off' period after any consent form has been signed.

MATTERS OF DEATH

3:4 Voluntary euthanasia – the issues

What are the main arguments for and against voluntary euthanasia?

Would voluntary euthanasia be the most humane way of allowing people to die with dignity or would it be the first step towards creating a society in which people, especially the elderly, no longer mattered? Euthanasia divides people into two clear camps on these questions. The Pro-Life Alliance is strongly opposed to euthanasia in any form. It defines euthanasia as: '… any action or omission intended to end the life of a patient on the grounds that his or her life is not worth living.' EXIT argues that voluntary euthanasia would be: '… a good death brought about by a doctor providing drugs or an injection to bring a peaceful end to the dying process.'

EXIT argues for living wills to be made legally binding, as they are in the Netherlands. A living will is a written, and witnessed, statement that a person wishes to die when their illness reaches a certain unbearable point. The Pro-Life Alliance does not believe that any person should be able to end their life prematurely.

> The goal of palliative care [pain control] is the achievement of the best quality of life for patients and their families.
>
> … THE WORLD HEALTH ORGANISATION, 1990

Arguments for voluntary euthanasia

- Everyone should have the right to decide whether their life should end. This is, perhaps, the most important and basic of all human rights.
- Everyone has the right to end their life in true dignity. Too often, life ends in a most undignified way and it is this that people dread as much as the pain that they experience.
- Once there is no hope left for a person's recovery, the quality of their life goes downhill. It is better to die before this happens. The quality of life is far more important than how long it lasts.
- Sometimes we treat animals better than we treat human beings. We put animals down before their pain becomes too great, so why not humans?
- Ending a life through euthanasia saves relatives and friends from unnecessary strain and anxiety.

Arguments against voluntary euthanasia

- There is always a hope for a recovery against the odds. A wrong diagnosis can sometimes be made.
- With the growth of the hospice movement and the development of modern drugs, no one needs to die in acute pain.
- Voluntary euthanasia would place an intolerable strain on elderly people and open them to pressure from relatives.
- God alone has the right to decide when anyone should die. All religions are strongly opposed to euthanasia for this reason.
- Euthanasia is nothing more than murder under another name.
- Euthanasia would compel doctors to break the Hippocratic Oath, which calls on them to provide the highest standards of care in the interests of their patients at all times (*see quotation*).

> I will use treatment to help the sick according to my ability and judgement, but never with a view to injury and wrongdoing. Neither will I administer a poison to anybody when asked to do so, nor will I suggest such a course … . But I will keep pure and holy both my life and my art.
>
> … HIPPOCRATIC OATH

✓ Exam tip
In the case of euthanasia and other social topics, candidates must know both sides of the argument. You should look in the newspapers for current examples. New and different circumstances are always arising. Use relevant and up-to-date information in your answers.

! Think about …
Do you think that there are some situations in which it might be difficult to argue **AGAINST** euthanasia? Give **TWO** examples to support your argument.

▲ Society is still trying to work out its attitude to euthanasia.

Tasks

1. a. Under what circumstances do you think a life-support machine should be turned off?
   b. If this happens do you think this is euthanasia?
   c. Who do you think should make the final decision: the courts, the relatives or the doctors?
2. Can you imagine a situation in which life for you was no longer worth living and had no meaning? What would that situation be?
3. Write **TWO** sentences about living wills.

SUMMARY

1 The arguments in favour of voluntary euthanasia are based on a person's right to decide when to die; their right to die in dignity and the strain placed on others by the continuation of their condition.

2 The arguments against voluntary euthanasia centre on the belief that God alone can decide when a person should die; the Hippocratic Oath, which compels doctors always to save life; and the hospice movement being able to offer effective palliative care at the end of a person's life.

MATTERS OF DEATH

3:5 Suicide

Why do so many people take their own lives and where can they turn for help?

Suicide – the facts

Suicide is a sad occurrence in modern life. Many people take their own life each year. Look at the statistics:

- About 1200 people in the world take their own lives each day. This works out at a suicide every 1.5 minutes.
- Men are more likely than women to kill themselves.
- The most vulnerable age group for suicide is between the ages of 20 and 45. In recent years, however, the number of suicides by teenagers has increased dramatically. These suicides are often linked with a breakdown in relationships with parents, being bullied at school or failure in school exams.
- About 10 per cent of people who fail in their attempt to take their own life later succeed in doing so. Because a person has failed to take their own life does not mean that they will not try again later – unless the reason for their suicide attempt is dealt with.

Suicide – the reasons

Suicide is a most extreme human act and people are usually driven to it by powerful reasons. Amongst the most common reasons are:

- money worries – personal or business
- loneliness – perhaps the death of a loved one; this is especially the case for elderly people whose partner has died
- redundancy – leading to long-term unemployment and no prospect of finding other work
- divorce – the loss of a family, break-up of a relationship, problems over access to children
- old age – the loss of physical or mental faculties; in 2002, a couple in their late fifties locked up the pub they owned, left a note saying they could not face growing old and simply disappeared; they were later found dead in a fume-filled car
- depression – illness, alcohol and drug abuse.

Suicide is often a 'cry for help'. This means that the person hopes they will be stopped, or discovered, before it is too late. Perhaps they have tried to tell someone about their problem and have not been taken seriously. Suicide, or attempted suicide, is often a desperate attempt to make people listen.

The Samaritans

The Samaritans is the main charity in the UK working with people considering suicide. In 1953, an Anglican priest, Chad Varah, set up The Samaritans after he discovered that many people were attempting to take their lives in his East London parish. To begin with he publicised a phone number in his own church that people could ring, day or night, for help. He soon found himself completely overwhelmed by the number of calls he received. He began to realise the true extent of the problem of self-destruction and the lack of any help that people could contact immediately. These were people 'at the end of their tether' and in need of help there and then.

This was the beginning of a charity called The Samaritans – a name taken deliberately from the story told by Jesus of the Good Samaritan (Luke 10.25–37). The Samaritans is not a Christian organisation, although many of its workers are Christians. In the telephone conversations that workers have with people they are not allowed to mention their religious faith.

Today there are branches of The Samaritans in most cities of the UK – over 200 in total. The telephones are staffed by volunteers who are ready to lend a listening ear to anyone in trouble. Strict anonymity is maintained between volunteer and client. Volunteers are only known by their first names and are expressly forbidden to enter into a close relationship with those who phone. Each year over 2 500 000 calls are made to The Samaritans in the UK and the number is increasing steadily.

> *Volunteers have to resist their natural impulse to solve some desperate cases by giving material help and comfort … they have to accept that when a client swears to phone the next day they will often break their word … they have to accept that weeks, and even months, may be spent on a case without a word of gratitude … they must remember that a person they have helped will often not even remember their name. The volunteer will find from bitter experience that he or she is often what they choose to be – faceless, nameless, just a voice or an ear on the end of a phone and nothing else.*
>
> **… SAMARITAN VOLUNTEER**

> *In His hand is every living soul and the breath of all mankind.*
>
> **... THE TANAKH (JOB 12.10)**

IMPORTANT WORDS

Samaritan; a member of an organisation that counsels people in distress

Suicide; the taking of one's own life, intentionally, without any assistance from someone else

Tasks

1. Write down **THREE** reasons why someone might try to take their own life.

2. a. Who are The Samaritans?
   b. Where did their name come from?
   c. What work do The Samaritans do?

3. a. Do you think that each person has the right to take their own life? Give **TWO** reasons for your answer.
   b. If a friend told you that they were thinking of taking their own life, how would you try to help them?

SUMMARY

1 Many people, young and old, try to take their own lives.

2 There may be many reasons for a person to attempt suicide – including money worries, loneliness, divorce, old age and school problems. Suicide is often a 'cry for help'.

3 The Samaritans is the leading organisation that tries to help people thinking of taking their own lives. It runs a strictly anonymous telephone contact service. The Samaritans receive over 2 500 000 calls each year.

▲ Very often The Samaritans is all that stands between a person and the taking of their own life.

MATTERS OF DEATH

3:6 Christianity and matters of death

What is the teaching of Christianity about euthanasia and suicide?

Euthanasia

> *Euthanasia is a temptation, in effect, to take the life of a man under the false pretext of giving him a pleasant and quiet death, so as not to see him continue a hopeless life of atrocious agony. Without the consent of the person euthanasia is murder. His consent would make it suicide. Morally this is a crime which cannot become legal by any means.*
>
> **... POPE PIUS VI**

All of the main Christian Churches have gone on record to oppose euthanasia, although there are many individual Christians who hold a different opinion. Christians also oppose suicide, though it is no longer the serious sin in the eyes of most Churches that it was held to be until the late 1950s.

The Christian Churches see their role as bringing the light and love of Jesus to everyone – young and old, fit and unwell. As Jesus himself showed, the work of his followers is to show God's love to those in need. This means helping the handicapped, the sick and the elderly to live as normal a life as possible. All life is sacred as human beings were made 'in the image of God' and are special and unique. Euthanasia would end the lives of frail and vulnerable people. In a real sense it is the frail, the vulnerable and the handicapped who are very special to God and in desperate need of being shown His love.

The Church cannot contemplate supporting euthanasia because:

- It does not show a true respect for God, the creator of all life. Human beings ignore God's laws at their peril.
- God created human beings with true worth and dignity. To kill a human being as if the person were just an animal is a grave sin.
- Euthanasia is murder so breaks one of the Ten Commandments (Exodus 20:13).

Even though doctors sometimes withhold treatment from a patient to hasten death, that is not legally considered to be euthanasia. Pain-killers, used to lessen pain, may also hasten death but this 'law of double-effect' is as far as doctors should go. The only exception to this is when a life-support machine is turned off – when a person is certified as being brain-dead. Otherwise, people must be looked after lovingly in the time leading up to their death, with their spiritual as well as their physical and emotional needs being met. It is a very important Christian belief that no one should have to die without being surrounded by the love of those who really care.

Suicide

In the past, the Christian Church took a very strong line against suicide, seeing it as nothing more than self-murder. Believing all life, and especially human life, to be a gift from God, suicide is seen to be to be a serious sin. The Roman Catholic Church has called it a 'mortal' sin in the past and serious enough to prevent the person from entering heaven. Catholics who took their own lives could not receive the blessing of a church funeral or be buried in consecrated (sacred) ground.

Today, though, all Churches take a more sympathetic line realising that many people live, and die, under great and intolerable pressure. They are committing suicide only out of great unhappiness and not because of wickedness. Many Christians are amongst those who volunteer to help with The Samaritans in the hope that they can persuade the suicidal that life is, after all, worth living.

▼ Christians believe that they, like Jesus, cannot escape suffering.

▲ Christians believe that the sufferings of this world, no matter how great, are less important than the joys of the world to come.

> *Your eyes saw my unformed limbs; they were all recorded in Your book.*
>
> **... THE TANAKH (PSALM 139.16)**

Exam tip
When writing an answer it is very important to select the important points you wish to make. Read the question carefully and identify the key points/words before you put pen to paper.

Tasks
1. a. What does the Christian Church see its main role to be today?
   b. How might this prevent it from accepting the use of euthanasia in modern society?
2. a. Write down **THREE** reasons why the Christian Church cannot accept euthanasia.
   b. What do you think might be **ONE** reason why a Christian today might feel that euthanasia is acceptable?
3. Describe in your own words the Christian attitude to suicide.

IMPORTANT WORDS
Law of double-effect; where drugs administered to a terminally ill patient to help with a condition may have the side effect of hastening their death

SUMMARY

❶ All Christian Churches are opposed to euthanasia. They believe that only God can give and end human life.

❷ The Churches believe that euthanasia does not show true respect for God, the Creator, or for the true dignity and worth of human beings. Euthanasia is seen as murder. Some Christians, though, argue for euthanasia on the grounds that it is the most humane course of action.

❸ In the past, the Church was strongly opposed to suicide, but its attitude is more sympathetic today. It recognises that many people are living their lives under impossible pressure. Many Christians work as Samaritans.

MATTERS OF DEATH

3:7 Judaism and Islam, and matters of death

What do Judaism and Islam teach about euthanasia and suicide?

■ JUDAISM

> *A season is set for everything, a time for every experience under heaven: A time for being born and a time for dying.*
>
> ... **THE TANAKH (ECCLESIASTES 3.1–2)**

Caring for the elderly. The Jewish Scriptures make it clear that the elderly should be respected and honoured. If possible, Jews try to look after their old people within the family, but there are homes to care for them if the family cannot do so. There are many home services, including Jewish Care, to meet the needs of the elderly.

▲ Jewish people often put up tapestries or stained-glass windows in memory of those who have died.

Euthanasia. Judaism does not support euthanasia. Life is such a great blessing from God that everything must be done to preserve it. In the Torah there are 613 laws and all but three of them can be broken in order to preserve life – the exceptions are murder, incest and idolatry. The Jewish Scriptures are very clear – it is God alone who decides when we are born and God who decides when we will die. There is an old Jewish saying that three people are involved in the conception of every baby – the mother, the father and God. Just as God is there at the beginning of life, so He is there at the end. Euthanasia would be playing God. Judaism does allow, however, for a life-support machine to be turned off if someone's life has all but ended. Keeping people alive artificially is also against the will of God.

Suicide. Believing in God as the creator of all life is at the heart of Judaism. So, too, is the belief that God gave human beings the freedom to make real decisions for themselves. This understanding extends to suicide. Although Judaism does not agree with suicide, individual Jews are often understanding about it. However, most Jews believe that God's greatest gift to them – the Torah – was given so that the Jews might live. The religion does not allow the normal burial rites to be carried out for those who have taken their own life or for them to be buried close to other people.

■ ISLAM

> *Nor can a soul die except by Allah's leave, the term being fixed as by writing.*
>
> ... **THE QUR'AN (3.145)**

Caring for the elderly. Muslim families consider it to be their responsibility to care for their elderly relatives. Apart from prayer, there is no greater religious duty. Muslim parents expect to be looked after by their children until they die.

Euthanasia. Muslims believe that every soul was created by Allah. Those who are going through prolonged physical pain remember that what happens in this life is a test for the coming Day of Judgement. Islam does not allow for any situation in which a life might be thought not to be worth living. Muslims must know that everything that happens to them in this life is part of the will of Allah. One of the 99 names of Allah is 'the Compassionate One'. This means that He is fully aware of all the trials and troubles through which believers pass. Muslims must accept this and not try to find an easy way out – which is what euthanasia would provide.

Suicide. Muslim law (the Shariah) lists the situations in which the taking of life is permissible and these do not include either euthanasia or suicide.

The events of 11 September 2002 showed that Muslim extremists do not regard the deliberate ending of one's life, when part of a jihad (holy war), to be suicide. However, they are the minority and most Muslims abide by the words of the Prophet Muhammad, who said that anyone who commits suicide will not be shown mercy on the Day of Judgement.

> *There was a man ... who had an affliction that taxed his patience, so he took a knife, cut his wrist and bled to death. Upon this God said: "My subject hastened his end. I deny him paradise."*
>
> ... **THE PROPHET MUHAMMAD, HADITH**

! Think about ...

Both Judaism and Islam believe in a compassionate God who cares for them. How do you think they reconcile this with the fact that many people end their life in pain and distress?

Tasks

1. a. What does Judaism teach about the value of life?
   b. How does Judaism show the great value it places on human life?
2. Why are Muslims strongly opposed to euthanasia?
3. What is the Muslim attitude to suicide?

IMPORTANT WORD

Shariah; all the laws of God concerning human activities found in the Qur'an

SUMMARY

1. Judaism and Islam both teach that children should look after their parents in old age. Judaism does accept that sometimes this might not be possible and that others might need to carry out the task. Looking after the elderly is a family obligation in Islam.

2. Both Judaism and Islam strongly oppose euthanasia – it is against the will of God. Many Jews, though, are sympathetic to those who have taken their own lives – a practice that is strongly deplored in Islam.

▲ The terrorists who bombed the World Trade Centre in New York claimed to be acting on behalf of Islam; yet, Shariah law forbids suicide.

MATTERS OF DEATH

3:8 Hinduism, Sikhism and Buddhism, and matters of death

What do Hinduism, Sikhism and Buddhism teach about euthanasia and suicide?

Hinduism, Sikhism and Buddhism all believe in reincarnation and this has a great bearing on their attitudes to euthanasia and suicide.

HINDUISM

> *The one who tries to escape from the trials of life by committing suicide will suffer even more in the next life.*
>
> ... YAJUR VEDA (40–43)

Caring for the elderly. The teaching of Hinduism is that each believer should treat their mother and father as gods.

Euthanasia and suicide. As all life is given by the Supreme Spirit it is up to Him to decide when each life should end. Respect and support must be given to everyone who is ill until their time comes to die naturally. To help someone else to die, as in euthanasia, would be to attract bad karma and cause suffering in future rebirths. Some Hindus would accept suicide if it were carried out for a religious reason, but the Scriptures do not support this. In the past, Hindu widows used to throw themselves on to the funeral pyres of their husbands and die with them. Although this practice, called 'suttee', has been outlawed since 1829 it still takes place in some country areas of India from time to time.

SIKHISM

Caring for the elderly. Sikhism teaches that the sick and elderly should be cared for by their family.

Euthanasia and suicide. Like most other religions, Sikhism teaches that life is a gift from God. It also teaches that the sick and elderly should be cared for with love, although it does not believe that life should be extended artificially. Some Sikhs argue that there is a place for euthanasia if someone wishes to die and is placing a great burden on other members of the family.

BUDDHISM

> *We have to look at the problem from the point of view of the ill person. Is the mind still awake, alert, capable of thinking and reasoning? If yes, it is of capital importance to let that person live.*
>
> ... DALAI LAMA, TIBETAN BUDDHIST LEADER

Caring for the elderly. In traditional Buddhist countries the elderly are highly valued for their wisdom and the way they have passed the religious traditions on to their children. They are also an example to others in another way: old people show that life itself is fragile and temporary. This is a very important lesson for all Buddhists to learn. Because of the way that they have given themselves to help others throughout their lives, the elderly must always be treated with great respect and care.

Euthanasia and suicide. It is a basic Buddhist belief that they should not harm any living thing (ahimsa). This is stated by the first of the Five Precepts. The motive for any action is as important to a Buddhist as the action itself.

As far as euthanasia is concerned, the question it raises is whether a person is trying to avoid responsibility for the elderly person or is acting in that person's own best interests. Each case needs to be considered on its merits. Along with other believers in reincarnation, it is the clear teaching of Buddhism that the body is little more than a shell and is unimportant. It is the progress of the soul towards enlightenment that is the great concern.

> *We may carry our mothers on one shoulder and our fathers on the other, and attend to them even for a hundred years but still the favour we have received from our parents will be far from paid back.*
>
> ... ANGUTTARA NIKAYA (VOL 1.61–2)

▲ All Hindus hope their body can be burned on the banks of the River Ganges, so that the soul can enter straight into heaven.

IMPORTANT WORDS

Ahimsa; the belief that Buddhists should be non-violent towards all forms of life; this is the first of the Five Precepts

Karma; the results of an action that are carried forward into the next life in both Hinduism and Buddhism

Tasks

1. Give **TWO** reasons why Hinduism is opposed to euthanasia.
2. Give **ONE** reason why some Sikhs are opposed to euthanasia and **ONE** reason why some Sikhs might be in favour.
3. Which Buddhist beliefs form the background to Buddhist teachings about euthanasia?
4. What problem is likely to be caused by euthanasia for anyone who believes in reincarnation?

Think about …

Look at the quote from the Anguttara Nikaya. More than one religion teaches that children owe an enormous debt to their parents and should spend the rest of their lives trying to pay it back. What do you think?

SUMMARY

1 Hinduism is strongly opposed to euthanasia as it attracts bad karma and affects the next rebirth of the soul.

2 Sikhism does not believe that euthanasia should be the normal course of action, although it is not totally opposed to it.

3 Buddhism teaches that each request for euthanasia should be judged on its own merits, but taking life is against the First Precept.

MATTERS OF DEATH

✓ Exam help ...

When looking at 'matters of death' it is very important to be aware of the importance of these topics for religious believers. All religions stress the importance of treating the elderly with love and respect. This is particularly important as the end of a person's life approaches. Euthanasia is one of the most controversial issues of modern life. You must be aware of the arguments for and against euthanasia and particularly the reasons why most religions are strongly opposed to it.

1.a. What is a hospice?

b. What is distinctive about the care that hospices offer?

1.a. In the Middle Ages a hospice offered refreshment to travellers/they were largely run by monks and nuns and looked after the sick and elderly/the modern hospice movement began at the start of the twentieth century/Dr Cicely Saunders founded a hospice in London in the 1960s – now there are many in the UK and across the world/looks after the terminally ill at the end of their lives/offers care to all, irrespective of religion.

b. Hospices exist to relieve pain, to help people face up to death, to care for the mental and emotional pain of friends and relatives/specialise in pain control (palliative care)/offer mainly short-term care because of pressure on shortage of beds/often work with Macmillan nurses offering care in home.

2.a. What is euthanasia?

b. How might a person's religious belief affect the way that they feel about euthanasia?

2.a. Forms of euthanasia: involuntary, voluntary, passive, active. Euthanasia means 'happy or easy death'/also 'mercy killing' – the premature ending of a life which has become intolerable through illness/euthanasia is illegal in the UK, but legal in the Netherlands. EXIT – society committed to making euthanasia legal in the UK.

b. All world religions are opposed to euthanasia:

Christianity: only God can determine death/distinction between passive euthanasia (withholding treatment) and active euthanasia (giving a lethal injection)/no wish to prolong suffering.

Judaism: life is a gift from God/people are in God's hands/God decides when life begins and ends/some Jews accept passive euthanasia, but active euthanasia is not allowed.

Islam: totally rejects idea of euthanasia/all suffering comes from Allah to test and strengthen faith/Allah decides how long a person should live.

Hinduism: suffering is the result of karma/people cannot escape its consequences and must live through it/if suffering is ended prematurely this has consequences for next rebirth.

Sikhism: nothing must be allowed to interfere with God's will/suffering must be seen through to end/but some Sikhs insist that the quality of life is more important than its length.

Buddhism: rebirth takes place at time of conception/euthanasia would interfere with reincarnation/also against First Precept, which forbids the taking of life/might relieve immediate pain, but karma determines that the pain would be experienced elsewhere.

Conclusion – euthanasia is against the principles at the heart of every major world religion.

CHAPTER 4
Drug abuse

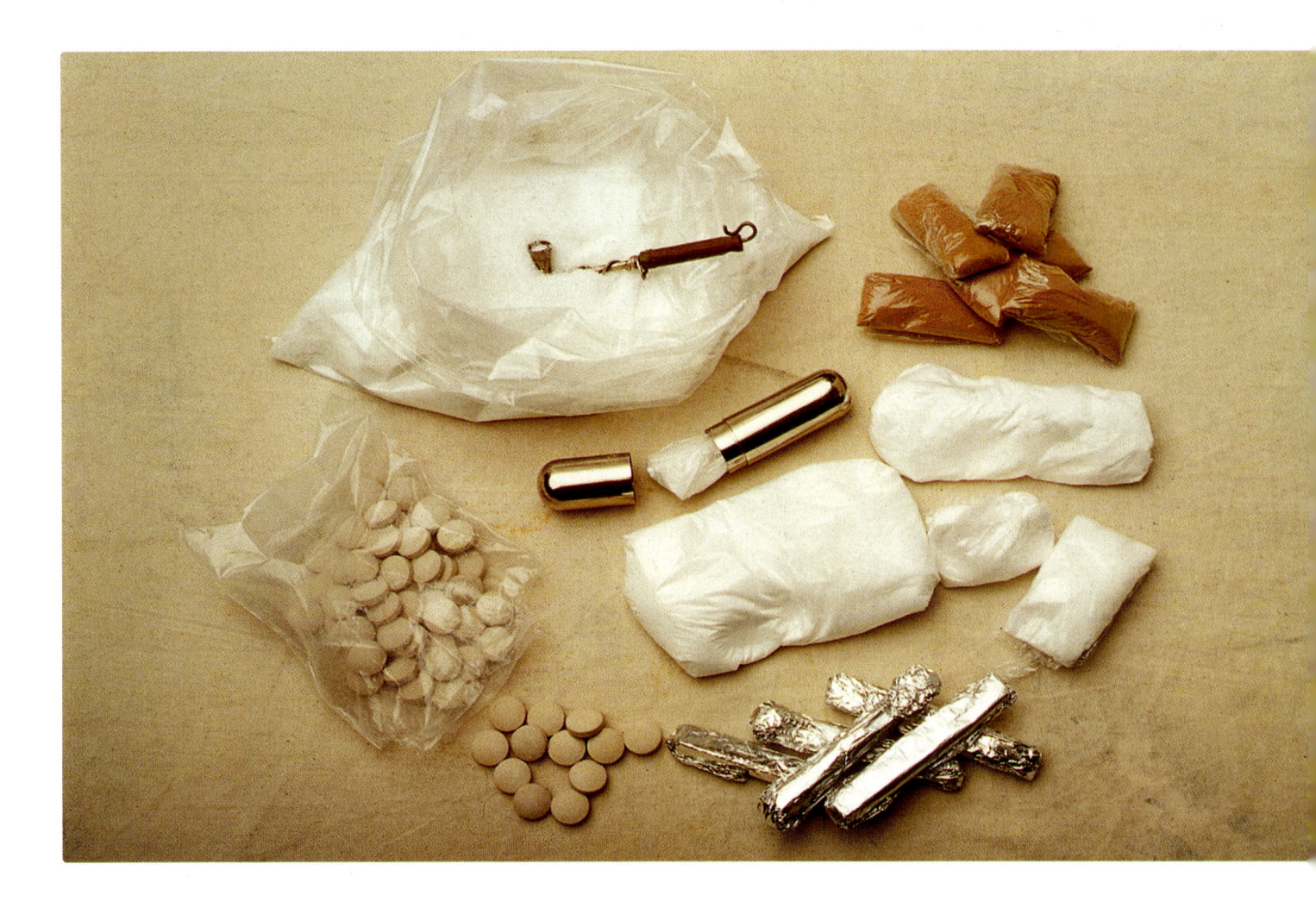

The taking of illegal drugs is a massive social problem. Religious and non-religious people share the concern that is felt at the havoc that over-drinking and drug abuse is causing in many individual lives and families. Any discussion of drugs must take place against the background of understanding what drugs we are talking about and the different effects they have on the people who take them. A clear distinction must be drawn between Class A drugs, Class B drugs, alcohol and smoking. As you consider the implications of the information in this section, there are important things that you will need to bear in mind.

- Taking drugs of any kind into the body questions the attitude that people have to their own bodies. Are they free to do as they like with it and abuse it or does it belong in some way to God? The five world religions give a very clear answer to this question. They teach that individuals have their bodies on loan from God and they are answerable to Him for the way they look after them. Bhuddists feel the body should be treated with care and the mind should be clear in order to meditate.

- Abusing the body has physical, emotional and spiritual consequences. Anything that alters a person's state of consciousness, if only for a short time, has serious spiritual consequences. For this reason, some religions are opposed to the drinking of alcohol, as well as to the taking of illegal substances. Worshipping God requires a clear head and a steady heart. It is impossible to worship or meditate if the body is under the influence of alcohol or any illegal substances. Islam, Sikhism and Buddhism all agree that the only spiritually mature way of life is that of total abstinence.

DRUG ABUSE

4:1 Drugs

What are the main drugs and how do they affect the human body?

> *There is a great deal of difference between dependent heroin injectors, occasional cannabis smokers and the weekend users of dance drugs. It is almost impossible to find out exactly why one person never tries drugs, another uses them occasionally and a third person is addicted before they reach the age of 20.*
>
> **... A MEDICAL WORKING PARTY**

What is a drug?

A 'drug' is any substance that is taken deliberately into the body to bring about a change in how we feel or alter how the body functions. The drugs that are not prescribed by a doctor can be divided into two categories.

1. **Legal drugs.** Alcohol and tobacco are the two most widely used legal drugs. In this country, over 90 per cent of the population drink alcohol regularly and about 30 per cent of adults smoke. Tens of thousands of people die each year as a direct result of using these two drugs, through such diseases as lung cancer and cirrhosis of the liver. Millions of people are addicted to alcohol or nicotine.

2. **Illegal drugs.** Far fewer people use illegal drugs, such as cocaine, heroin and marijuana regularly, than use alcohol and tobacco. Consequently, fewer people die through using illegal drugs, but they are much more addictive than alcohol and tobacco.

The thing that binds these legal and illegal drugs together is that they are all used for 'recreational' purposes. There is no medical reason for people to take them: they are taken for the 'buzz' they give. They are often linked with other 'recreational' activities, such as socialising in a pub, attending a party or going to a rave. There are also people who take drugs on their own, especially when they are addicted. Many people, for instance, trying to give up smoking, find that this is most difficult when they are with other smokers. The same applies to drugs.

Recreational drugs

Recreational drugs have been around, and used, for a very long time. There are records of organised drinking houses in ancient Babylon 3000 years ago. Drinking alcohol is sanctioned by most religions, except Islam and Sikhism where it is banned because of its undesirable side-effects. Often, as in Judaism and Christianity, drinking alcohol is an important part of special services and festivals.

Tobacco was brought to Europe by Christopher Columbus in the fifteenth century, although smoking cigarettes did not catch on until the twentieth century. Smoking the leaves of the cannabis plant has been practised in India and the Arab world for thousands of years. It has been used in Hindu rituals for a long time. It only became popular in the UK and the USA around the 1950s with the hippie and beat generations. The coca leaf, the basis of cocaine, was chewed by the Peruvian Indians and was used for medical reasons in the UK from the 1850s. Opium was also used in Britain in the 1850s. LSD and Ecstasy are both inventions of the twentieth century. Strangely, in some places people used drugs because they were poor and in other areas because they had enough money to pay for them.

Why do people take drugs?

The taking of illegal drugs exploded from the 1970s onwards. There would appear to be several possible reasons for this.

1. To escape from the boredom of life.
2. To experiment – many people who become addicted to drugs begin the habit in their teenage years.
3. To show rebellion – most young people know what the reaction of their parents would be if they knew what they were doing.
4. To find out what it feels like – being curious and wanting to have new experiences.
5. Peer pressure – research shows that most young people are introduced to drugs for the first time by their friends or other young people. Everyone seems to be doing it and so they go along with it.
6. Addiction.

IMPORTANT WORDS

Alcohol;	a liquid generated by the fermentation of sugar and forming the intoxicating element of fermented liquors
Illegal drug;	a narcotic substance, especially an addictive one
Recreational drug;	a drug that is used for non-medical reasons – as a social habit

Tasks

1. What is a drug?
2. Describe the **TWO** categories into which drugs can be divided.
3. a. What are recreational drugs?
   b. Write about **THREE** recreational drugs.

SUMMARY

1 A drug is any chemical substance that, when taken, brings about actual changes in the body. Recreational or social drugs can be divided into those that are legal and those that are not.

2 Whilst LSD and Ecstasy are fairly recent inventions, most drugs have been around for a long time.

3 There are many possible reasons why a person might start taking drugs.

▼ Alcohol is the most widely used of the recreational drugs.

DRUG ABUSE

4:2 Legal drugs

Which drugs are legal and are they harmless?

> *Alcohol can give pleasure and cause harm. It is used in celebration, socialisation and relaxation; it can also be enjoyed for its taste ... all Methodists should seriously consider the claims of total abstinence and make a personal commitment to either total abstinence or responsible drinking.*
>
> **... THE METHODIST CONFERENCE, 1987**

There are three drugs that are socially acceptable, and widely used, in modern society.

Alcohol – the facts

- Contrary to popular belief, alcohol is not a stimulant – it depresses the central nervous system. It affects a person's judgement, reduces their inhibitions and slows their reflexes even when only taken in very small quantities. This is why the amount a person can take and still drive legally has been steadily reduced.
- Men drink an average of eight pints of beer a week and women three pints. Men can absorb alcohol into their bodies far better than women. This means that often women are affected by their alcohol intake far quicker than men.
- Industry loses about £2 billion a year and 10 million working days through the after-effects of drinking. Alcohol is also responsible for many accidents in the workplace.
- 25 per cent of men admitted to hospital have alcohol-related problems and drinking costs the National Health Service around £200 million a year. Violence against doctors and nurses has increased sharply and is mostly due to the effects of alcohol. Saturday nights between 11pm and 2am account for over 75 per cent of all violence in hospital Accident and Emergency departments.
- Alcohol is a major factor in some 30 000 deaths a year in the UK. 20 per cent of all road accidents are caused by people being over the drink-driving limit and 65 000 people are prosecuted or cautioned each year for breaking the law. Advertising campaigns, especially over the Christmas break, seem incapable of reducing this figure.

▼ Although a drug, alcohol is a widely accepted part of many people's lives in the UK today.

- 10 per cent of drinkers develop a serious drinking problem leading, in many cases, to alcoholism. Alcoholism is a disease. It is also a killer leading to cirrhosis of the liver and other serious health problems. Over 50 per cent of people who commit violent acts have been drinking. In the case of domestic violence the figure is higher.

Nicotine – the facts

- The government takes more money in tobacco taxes than it does from alcohol – but only just! In the world, 18 per cent of people smoke, but in the UK the figure is around 30 per cent. Smoking is the greatest single cause of preventable death. The pleasurable element in smoking, nicotine, is highly addictive – as addictive as heroin.
- There are 300 harmful chemicals in a cigarette and these affect both the active and the passive smoker – the one who breathes in the fumes.
- About 90 per cent of the people who die from lung cancer and 75 per cent who die from bronchitis each year do so as a direct result of smoking. In total, smoking kills about 3 million people in the world a year – a staggering total of over 300 people a day!

Caffeine – the facts

- Caffeine occurs naturally in coffee and tea. It is an addictive drug that stimulates the central nervous system and provides an energy boost. Large doses increase the risk of heart attacks, as well as causing restlessness and sleeplessness.

! Think about ...

Why do you think so many people drink heavily and smoke when the health dangers of doing so have been well publicised? Provide **THREE** reasons to explain what appears to be very strange behaviour.

Tasks

1. Write down **THREE** reasons why drinking alcohol is such a popular pastime.
2. a. Write down **FIVE** facts about alcohol and drinking.
   b. Which fact surprises you most and why?
3. a. Write down **FIVE** facts about smoking.
   b. Which fact surprises you most and why?
4. It has been said that if tobacco and alcohol were discovered today they would soon be made illegal. What do you think? Give **TWO** reasons for your answer.

> The Christian ideal has been to refuse to expose life to actions or circumstances which carry with them high risks of harm … . It has been shown that smoking renders the individual prone to illness and premature death. It can therefore be argued that it is a denial of the goodness of created existence.
>
> **... CHURCH OF ENGLAND BRIEFING**

▲ Cigarette smoking is the main cause of lung cancer, the most common form of cancer in Britain.

SUMMARY

1 Alcohol is a depressant. Taken in any quantity it changes human behaviour considerably. Drinking alcohol heavily has serious long-term health consequences.

2 Smoking cigarettes has serious long-term health consequences. The nicotine content is highly addictive. Smoking affects the person smoking and anyone breathing in their smoke.

3 Caffeine occurs naturally in tea and coffee. Heavy consumption can have side effects.

DRUG ABUSE

4:3 Drugs in sport

Why is the use of drugs in sport a growing problem?

There has been a considerable interest recently in the media in the increased use of drugs by sportsmen and women to enhance their performance. Several leading athletes have been identified as drug-takers by official testing programmes. Some of them have been named, whilst others have been allowed to remain anonymous.

The use of drugs in sport is not new. In Ancient Greece mass spectator sport and rich prizes led to the development of 'professionalism' in sport. Bribing and cheating were considered to be normal activities and some competitors used what were believed to be performance-enhancing substances, such as mushrooms and plant extracts. Whenever sport is about reward, rather than personal enjoyment, some competitors will seek to gain an unfair advantage over their rivals. Many sports list banned substances and operate systematic testing programmes to discourage drug use.

Different drugs have different effects, so a substance banned in one sport may be acceptable in another. Anabolic steroids, which help build muscle, could make an athlete stronger or faster; this could be an advantage to a sprinter or a shot putter, but a distinct disadvantage to an archer or a long-distance runner. The main downside is the effect that steroids have on the body. They cause the premature accumulation of fats in the arteries and death can result from the effects of these on the heart and blood vessels. Steroids can also cause people to break into sudden and fiery rages (called 'roid rage'). These have occasionally led to vicious attacks on other people.

IT'S A FACT

In 2000, scientists at Aberdeen University discovered that some food supplements can produce high levels of nandrolone (a banned substance), when taken alongside excessive physical exercise. This led UK Athletics to overturn sporting bans that had been imposed on three athletes, including Linford Christie.

Some claim that athletes must have real talent to succeed if they are going to be outstanding and that drugs merely enhance these talents. In other words, there is no need for concern as long as everyone has access to them, as true talent will emerge at the top of the pile in the end. Others claim that taking drugs, in any form, is cheating. This is certainly the official view of the different sporting authorities, which carry out a constant war against those who take drugs. There are two problems with this.

1. Much drug testing is ineffective because careful planning by an athlete can ensure that traces of most drugs disappear from the body before testing can take place. The search continues for more efficient ways of carrying out testing.
2. The human body naturally produces some banned substances. This means that test results can never be 100 per cent certain.

> *Using chemicals to do what your body isn't capable of doing is cheating, but it is a form of cheating that is hidden and therefore it is a nasty form of cheating.*
>
> ... JOHN WHETTON, OLYMPIC ATHLETE

The issues involved

The use of performance-enhancing drugs has become a very important issue in sport. It has been pointed out that:

1. Sport ought to be a fair and above-board competition between highly skilled performers who achieve their results by natural ability and hard work. Drugs destroy all that sport really stands for.
2. Banned substances almost certainly cause long-term harm to an athlete's body. It is thought, for instance, that the premature and unexpected death of Florence Griffith Joyner ('Flo-Jo'), in 1998, was the result of taking drugs over many years.
3. The standards accepted in sport reflect the standards accepted in society generally. Taking drugs in any form is a way of interfering with nature – and breaking God's laws. Sports stars are heroes and role-models for millions of young people. Their example of drug abuse, or of rejecting drugs, could have a great effect on the behaviour of those who admire them.

IT'S A FACT

It was announced before the 2000 Sydney Olympics that tests would take place to look for erythropietin (EPO). Dozens of athletes withdrew from the Games.

▲ Florence Griffith Joyner was a top athlete in the 1990s. She died aged 38. Many people suspected that she used performance–enhancing drugs and her early death seemed to confirm this, although she never failed a drugs test.

> " The moral crusade against the use of drugs in sport, like most moral crusades, is surrounded by myth. One of the myths is that fans will not pay to see drug-aided athletes perform. A second myth is that using drugs means that athletes don't have to work hard for their achievements. It is undoubtedly true, nonetheless, that the idea of using performance enhancing drugs is deeply disturbing to a great many people.
>
> ... **NEW STATESMAN, SEPTEMBER 1998** "

Tasks

1. Give **TWO** ways in which the taking of banned substances might affect sport.

2. Write **TWO** sentences about anabolic steroids and the dangers they might present to those who take them.

3. Think of **TWO** arguments that might be put forward by someone arguing that the use of drugs in sport should be legalised and **TWO** arguments by someone who is opposed to the idea.

SUMMARY

1 Attempts to cheat at sport are not new. The use of drugs to enhance sporting performance is widespread.

2 Anabolic steroids increase body bulk and strength. They have short-term and long-term side effects. They can be detected. The taking of many drugs, though, can be masked and some cannot be detected at the moment.

3 One problem with detecting drug abuse is that the body naturally produces some banned substances.

4 Sporting authorities are constantly trying to find better ways of testing athletes for drugs.

DRUG ABUSE

4:4 Class A drugs

What are the main 'hard' drugs and what effects do they have on the body?

> *The world's drug trade has grown dramatically over the last decade and is now bigger than international trade in iron and steel and motor vehicles.*
>
> ... THE GUARDIAN, 26 JUNE 1997

In the UK, the Misuse of Drugs Act 1971 places drugs into three categories, although drugs have been outlawed at different times since 1971.

Class A: Cocaine, Ecstasy, LSD, morphine, heroin, opium – attracting a maximum 7-year term for possession and life imprisonment for supplying the drug to others.

Class B: Amphetamines, barbiturates, cannabis – maximum 5-year term for possession and up to 14 years for supplying the drug to others.

Class C: Anabolic steroids – maximum 2-year term for possession and up to 5 years for supplying the drug to others.

There are four main drugs in the Class A category and these are sometimes called 'hard' drugs.

1. **Heroin.** Heroin is a synthetic chemical derivative of morphine, which comes from the opium poppy. Heroin is most likely to be injected directly into a vein giving an immediate 'high'. It is very likely to lead to serious, and speedy, addiction with withdrawal being an intensely unpleasant and life-threatening procedure. It leads to intense diarrhoea, stomach cramps, headache, nausea, vomiting and convulsions.

2. **Cocaine.** Cocaine comes from the leaves of the coca plant, which is grown in the South American Andes. Cocaine is usually absorbed through the nose ('snorted') and is the worst of all drugs for addiction potential. 1 in every 6 people who take a snort will become addicts. Those addicted have a miserable existence. Finding the next dose of the drug is the only thing that matters in an addict's life.

3. **Ecstasy.** Ecstasy was freely available until 1977 when it became illegal. It was then associated with the rave dance scene, providing users with the energy to stay awake to dance all night. Several hundred thousand people in Britain and the USA now use the drug each week. Frequently, newspapers carry stories of young people dying after taking the drug. It causes the body temperature to rise and unless water or soft drinks are taken frequently a person may suffer from severe dehydration. In 2000, the Police Federation doubted whether Ecstasy should be a Class A drug.

4. **LSD.** LSD remains popular amongst those on the rave dance scene. It causes intense visual and audio sensations resulting in hallucinations. In 1954, when Aldous Huxley took a similar drug in a famous experiment he described the experience as similar to being present on the morning of the world's creation – experiencing the miracle of naked existence. Some users have very bad experiences with LSD and may unintentionally cause their own death by thinking that they can fly or perform other impossible physical feats. Over the years many people have died in this way.

The lure of drugs

During the 1980s there was an epidemic of heroin use in this country. The epidemic has continued into this century. There are now at least 60 000 heroin addicts and a much larger number who use the drug. Cocaine is now largely sold as 'crack' and the number of those using the drug has climbed steadily. It is thought that about £100 million each year is stolen to finance the drug habits of those who are serious users.

Tasks

1. a. Name **THREE** Class A drugs.
   b. What prison sentences can be passed for the possession and supplying of Class A drugs?
2. Write down **THREE** pieces of information about:
   a. heroin   b. cocaine
   c. Ecstasy   d. LSD.

! Think about ...

It is not always easy to determine a person's motives for the way they behave. The dangers of taking drugs, however, have been very widely publicised. What do you think are the main motives young people have for ignoring the dangers?

IT'S A FACT

The *Guardian* reported in 1997 that the largest drugs investigation known at the time spanned three continents and led to the seizure of £65 million worth of cocaine and cannabis as well as 44 arrests.

SUMMARY

1 UK law classifies drugs into A, B and C categories. Class A is the most serious category and carries the heaviest penalties for use and supplying.

2 Heroin, cocaine, LSD and Ecstasy are the most widely used Class A drugs. Heroin and cocaine are the most addictive of illegal drugs. LSD and Ecstasy are associated with the dance rave scene.

▼ Addiction to Class A drugs is very likely to lead to an early death.

DRUG ABUSE

4:5 Class B drugs

What are 'soft' drugs and what effect do they have on those who take them?

There are three main Class B drugs and these are often called 'soft' drugs.

1. **Barbiturates.** Barbiturates were widely used as sedatives in the early twentieth century and they were also used as a recreational drug for a time before their use for this purpose largely died out. They have the potential to be misused because they can produce an alcohol-like feeling of intoxication when taken. They can be highly addictive. Attempts to withdraw can result in epileptic fits. At one time in the 1970s, 2000 people were dying a year in the UK through misusing barbiturates.

2. **Amphetamines.** An amphetamine (also known as 'speed') is a stimulant that increases wakefulness and suppresses the appetite. However, even though some students use it to stay awake to revise for an exam, it actually reduces their ability to think clearly and so is counter-productive. Taking amphetamines can be followed by depression, sleeplessness and feelings of paranoia. Amphetamines can be taken by mouth, sniffed as a powder, smoked or injected. Short-term effects include increased heart rate and blood pressure, poor complexion and diarrhoea. Long-term use strains the heart and can lead to schizophrenia.

3. **Cannabis.** Cannabis comes from the marijuana plant. It is used in three main forms – the leaves (grass, pot), resin (hash) and liquid (cannabis oil). Cannabis oil became a Class A drug in 1994. Cannabis is usually mixed with tobacco and smoked. It produces a feeling of intense relaxation and will slow the body's reactions; making it dangerous to drive, for example. Cannabis takes longer to disappear from the body than alcohol and many drivers do not realise this. Some police authorities are talking about roadside testing for drugs as well as alcohol.

Cannabis has been associated with schizophrenia and reduced fertility in men. Cannabis can lead to addiction although the withdrawal symptoms are much milder than for other drugs. There was increased demand at the start of this century for a reclassification of cannabis as a Class C, rather than a Class B, drug. Many people believe that cannabis should be legalised because it is, they say, no more dangerous than alcohol and tobacco.

Should cannabis be legalised?
There is a widespread debate over whether cannabis should be decriminalised or even legalised.

Arguments for legalising cannabis

- The police waste a lot of time prosecuting people who use a largely harmless drug for their own use.
- If cannabis were legalised, those who supply the drug, and make fortunes from selling it, would be put out of business.
- People who are successfully prosecuted for using cannabis have a criminal record for what many feel should not be an offence.
- Cannabis is used by some people to counter the pain that they are suffering. Some people suffering from multiple sclerosis, for example, find it particularly helpful. Why should cannabis be difficult for them to obtain for their own private and medicinal use? In 2002, there were suggestions that cannabis might be available on prescription for those who need it medically.

Arguments against legalising cannabis

- Many believe that cannabis is a 'gateway' drug – one that can lead to taking other drugs.
- If cannabis were made legal, the market would be flooded and more people would end up smoking it. There are already over 5 million regular users.
- Even if cannabis is relatively harmless, it is still a drug. All drugs, including alcohol and cigarettes, are harmful to health and a waste of money.

IT'S A FACT

- Today amphetamines are the second most widely used illegal drug. Across the UK 13 per cent of 15–16-year-olds and 20 per cent of 16–29-year-olds have tried them.
- Cannabis is the most widely used illegal drug in the UK. 42 per cent of 15–16-year-olds have tried cannabis. Official Home Office figures show a third of adults in England and Wales have used the drug.
- In many parts of the country, police 'turn a blind eye' to those caught with small amounts of cannabis in their possession. In 2001, MP Jon Owen Jones argued, in a private member's bill, that cannabis should be available at places such as off licences!

▲ Taking drugs is strongly linked to the life-style of many young people.

Tasks

1. Write **THREE** sentences about each of the following:

   a. barbiturates **b.** amphetamines
   c. cannabis.

2. 'Cannabis should be legalised so that those who use it can no longer be criminalised.' Do you agree with this comment? Give **TWO** reasons to support your argument.

✓ Exam tip
If you are confronted by a question like 'Should cannabis be legalised?' you are being invited to present arguments for and against, before coming to your own conclusion. Remember to include a religious perspective.

IMPORTANT WORDS

Hard drugs; Class A drugs
Soft drugs; Class B drugs, such as cannabis

SUMMARY

❶ The three main Class B drugs are barbiturates, amphetamines and cannabis. Barbiturates are rarely used nowadays for recreational purposes, but a large part of drug-taking involves amphetamines and cannabis.

❷ The most hotly debated question relating to drugs is whether or not cannabis should be legalised. Some believe that it is a 'gateway' drug, but others maintain that it is largely harmless. Different police forces have different attitudes to those found with cannabis in their possession.

DRUG ABUSE

4:6 Christianity and drugs

What does Christianity teach about drinking alcohol, smoking and taking drugs?

> *Do not get drunk with wine, which will only ruin you.*
>
> ... THE BIBLE (EPHESIANS 5.18)

Christians say that the careful, medically directed use of drugs to heal is acceptable. Drugs are part of God's gift in creation. Christians support the ongoing search by scientists for new drugs to treat illness and disease more effectively. Even here, though, it is possible to become dependent on the very drugs that are intended to help – and that can be very serious. Each night, for instance, 4 million sleeping pills are taken by people in the UK and it is thought that at least 25 per cent of these people would find it very difficult to give them up – or to sleep without them. Their dependence is often more psychological than physical, but the problems of breaking their addiction are just as great.

Smoking

As you would expect, the Bible has nothing to say about smoking. Some Christians smoke, including many vicars. Generally Christians recognise the damage that smoking does to the body and believe it is more honouring to God to abstain.

Alcohol

During the nineteenth century, many Christian Churches taught their members to abstain from alcohol – to be teetotallers. The Methodist Church was at the forefront of this by preaching abstinence and making this a condition of church membership. This message was mainly based on an observation of the damage done to family and personal lives by heavy drinking. In the absence of any social services the Church was often left to pick up the pieces. Even today the Salvation Army requires all of its officers to be teetotal and not to smoke.

There are two broad Christian attitudes to drinking alcohol today.

1. There are some who believe it is better to abstain because of the damage that alcohol can do to people. Teetotalism has become increasingly rare, though, amongst the Christian community.

2. There are many who believe that alcohol is a gift from God and to be enjoyed by all – but only in moderation. The Old Testament highlights that the 'fruit of the vine' is a gift from God but also that it is only the foolish who drink too much. It explains that too much alcohol persuades people to do things of which they would normally be ashamed.

Drug-taking

The person whose life is dominated and ruined by drugs, whether alcohol, nicotine or illegal drugs, is a person whose life is falling apart. They may end up losing their job, their family, their home and their dignity. Eventually they may well lose their life. Jesus said it was people in such desperate need that he was chiefly concerned to help. He described his reason for coming to earth in these words:

> *People who are well do not need a doctor, but only those who are sick. I have not come to call respectable people, but outcasts.*
>
> ... THE BIBLE (MARK 2.17)

Anyone re-writing the parable of the Prodigal Son for today (Luke 15.11–32) might well cast the younger son as a drug addict!

Following the example of Jesus, Christians respond to the problems of drug taking with love and concern. The care given by Christians to drug addicts in many places is just the same as that given by people of other faiths and those of no faith. The motivation, though, is different. Many Christians would say that in helping those in need they are helping Christ. This is because Christ is in all people.

This helps people to understand the motivation of such people as Mother Teresa and Dame Cicely Saunders, both outstanding examples of Christian love in action. There are many others doing equally important work but who remain largely unknown.

> *Christians must face the serious scientific evidence about the harmful effects of drugs. A Christian's faith teaches him to use all things responsibly.*
>
> ... THE METHODIST CONFERENCE, 1987

> *Don't you know that your body is the temple of the Holy Spirit, who lives in you and who was given to you by God? You do not belong to yourselves but to God; he bought you for a price. So use your bodies for God's glory.*
>
> ... **THE BIBLE (1 CORINTHIANS 6.19–20)**

! Think about ...

Look at the quotation from 1 Corinthians 6.19–20. When Christians discuss smoking, alcohol and drugs, this verse is usually brought forward. What do you think it has to say on the subject?

IMPORTANT WORDS

Methodist Church; Protestant Church formed in the eighteenth century
Teetotalism; completely abstaining from drinking any alcohol

Tasks

1. a. Why do you think that the Salvation Army demands that its officers do not smoke or drink alcohol?
   b. Why do you think that it is does not allow its officers to do these things even 'in moderation'?
2. a. Do you think that it is realistic to expect people to drink alcohol in moderation?
   b. Why do you think so many people over-indulge?
3. Why do Christians have a motive for helping those with alcohol or drug-related problems?

SUMMARY

1. Some Christians are teetotallers. They do not drink because of the damage that alcohol can, and does, cause. The majority, though, drink in moderation.

2. Although many Christians smoke, it is generally disapproved of in the Christian community.

3. Christians have been at the forefront of those trying to help people whose lives have been ruined by taking drugs.

▼ The Salvation Army is one Christian organisation working amongst those on the fringes of society – a situation often brought about by drug abuse.

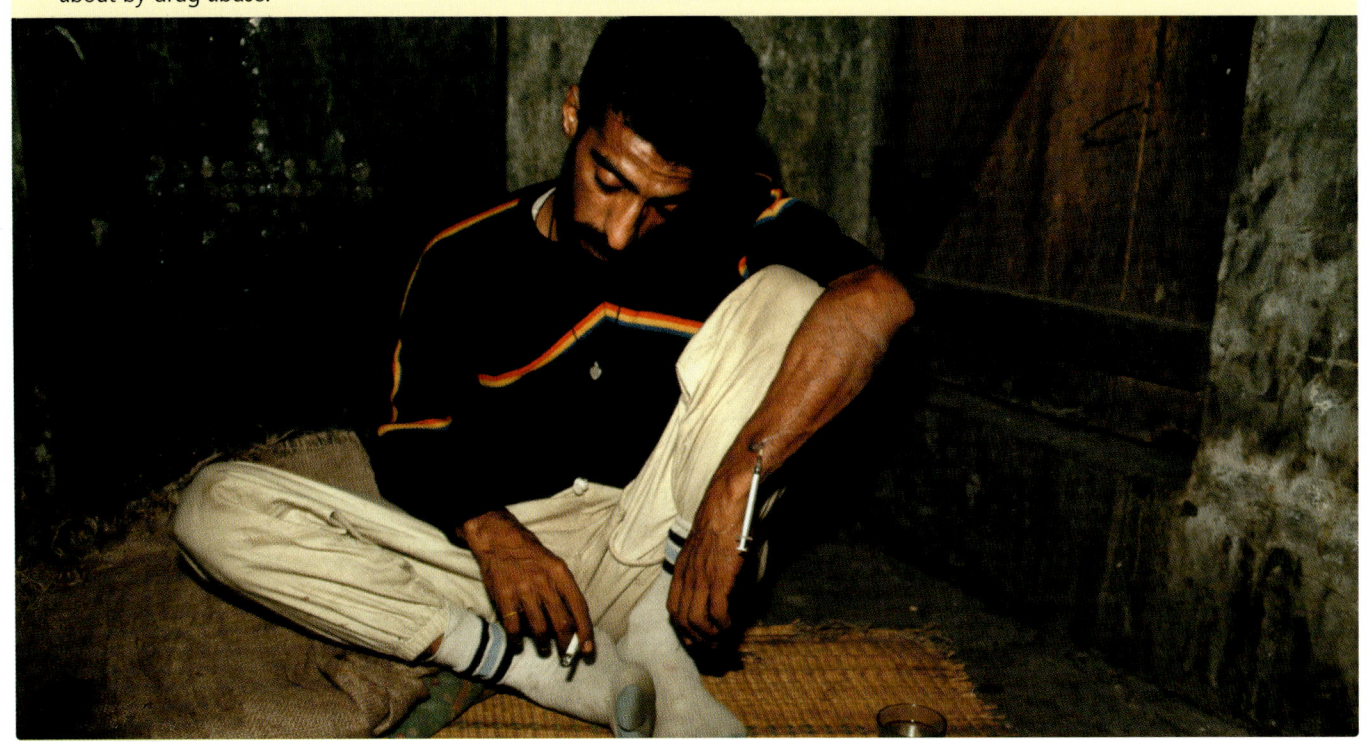

DRUG ABUSE

4:7 Judaism and Islam, and drugs

What is the teaching of Judaism and Islam on drug-taking?

■ JUDAISM

> *Wine enters, sense goes out; wine enters, secrets come out.*
>
> ... JEWISH SAYING

Smoking. Moses Maimonides, a great rabbi from the twelfth century, taught that no one has the right to put his own, or someone else's, life in danger by the way they behave. Another Jewish teacher told his followers that it is better to eat unkosher food than to put one's life in danger. Although many Jews smoke, the habit is strongly discouraged.

Alcohol. The Talmud, a Jewish holy book, says that there is 'no celebration without wine'. Certainly, most important Jewish celebrations are accompanied by the drinking of wine 'to loosen the spirit'. At the festival of Purim, the Talmud requires that Jews get a little tipsy to the point where they are not sure whether 'you are blessing Mordecai or cursing Haman'. Jews recognise, however, that wine clouds the judgement and the Talmud says that a rabbi should not give any spiritual advice if he has drunk alcohol.

Drug-taking. The Jewish teaching is that the body should always be treated with care and respect. Any form of self-abuse, such as injecting with drugs, breaks this teaching. Jewish teaching also lays a great emphasis on the need to have a clear mind, which is capable of reaching rational decisions. The taking into the body of any unnecessary chemical substances rules this out. A number of Jewish care organisations now run drug counselling and rehabilitation services.

■ ISLAM

> *Intoxicants, gambling and trying to foretell the future are the lures of Satan; if you wish to prosper you must keep away from these things.*
>
> ... THE QUR'AN (5.90)

Any substance that intoxicates is known in Arabic as 'khamr' and is forbidden to Muslims. Muslims cannot enter into wudu – the washing ritual before prayers – unless they are in full possession of their senses: without wudu they are forbidden to pray.

Smoking. Smoking is not forbidden to Muslims and millions do so. However, it would seem to be ruled out by the Muslim principles of not doing wrong to oneself or to others.

Alcohol. The prohibition against Muslims drinking alcohol is absolute. Whilst some Muslims argue that drinking in moderation is acceptable, that is not the teaching of the Qur'an. In countries ruled by strict Islamic governments, the penalty normally imposed on those who drink and display antisocial behaviour is flogging. The Prophet Muhammad said that the use of alcohol in medicine was an abomination to Allah: "Alcohol is not a medicine, but a disease."

Drug-taking. Whilst drug-taking under the supervision of a doctor is perfectly acceptable, Islam sees such substances as heroin, cocaine and marijuana as contrary to the spirit of the faith. They affect the human mind and destroy a body that Allah has created. To do this is a very serious sin. Drugs also offer the person who takes them a way of escaping from the pains and distresses of life – even though these have been sent by Allah to test and strengthen the faith of the person.

> **✓ Exam tip**
> It is important to be able to separate the teaching of different religions on the same subject. So, for instance, Judaism incorporates the drinking of wine in almost all of its religious ceremonies, but Islam is totally opposed to the drinking of alcohol at any time. Make sure you do not mix them up.

> **IMPORTANT WORDS**
>
> **Talmud;** major work covering all aspects of Jewish law
> **Wudu;** the Muslim washing ritual performed before prayers

Tasks

1. How is drinking wine an important part of the Jewish faith?
2. What is the Jewish attitude to drug-taking?
3. What is the Muslim attitude to all intoxicants, including alcohol?
4. Give **TWO** reasons why Muslims are expected not to take drugs.

SUMMARY

1 Drinking alcohol plays a very important role in the Jewish way of life – especially in its religious ceremonies.

2 Drug-taking is strictly outlawed in the teaching of both the Jewish and Muslim communities.

3 Drinking alcohol is strictly forbidden for any Muslim.

▼ The washing routine of wudu must precede the offering of prayers for every Muslim. It is strictly forbidden for any Muslim to come to wudu under the influence of any intoxicant.

DRUG ABUSE

4:8 Hinduism, Sikhism and Buddhism, and drugs

What do Hindus, Sikhs and Buddhists believe about taking drugs?

HINDUISM

> *He must not get wilfully addicted to any object or substance of self-gratification; he must try to overcome such dependence through will-power.*
>
> ... THE LAWS OF MANU, A HINDU HOLY BOOK

Smoking. Many Hindus smoke. The costly habit of smoking expensive brands of cigarette has become common in certain upper classes of Hindu society as they have been targeted by the manufacturers of these cigarettes. Men, in particular, seem to see it as a privilege to be involved in such activity. Smoking in the presence of one's elders in Hindu society, though, is believed by many to show a lack of respect.

Alcohol. Alcohol has been part of the Indian way of life for centuries. Modern Hindus tolerate the moderate drinking of alcohol. However, heavy drinking is a problem in many parts of India.

Drug-taking. Hindus believe that, used properly, drugs can be of enormous benefit. Drugs, especially opium (heroin) are grown in many parts of India and exported illegally to feed a worldwide demand for them. Whilst many Hindus condemn the taking of drugs they are used by many sadhus (holy men) as part of religious devotion. The ancient lawgiver, Manu, warned against any form of addiction *(see quotation)*.

SIKHISM

> *By drinking wine one loses sanity; one loses the power of discrimination and incurs God's displeasure.*
>
> ... AMAR DAS, THE THIRD SIKH GURU

Smoking. Sikhs look upon the body as a holy temple, which should be looked after with care. This applies to smoking tobacco. It clouds the mind and damages the lungs, the heart and other parts of the body. It is not encouraged.

Alcohol. Drinking any form of alcohol (and smoking) is forbidden for Khalsa muslims. Sikhs believe that alcohol damages and weakens the body. It also takes away a person's ability to think clearly.

Drug-taking. In Guru Nanak's day it was common for drugs to be taken. When the Guru had an audience with the emperor Babur he was offered a drink containing opium. He replied that he was 'hooked' on praising God. Sikhs are asked to make sure that they are carrying no alcohol, cigarettes or drugs when they enter a gurdwara.

BUDDHISM

> *I undertake the rule of training to refrain from drugs or drinks which tend to cloud the mind.*
>
> ... THE FIFTH PRECEPT OF BUDDHISM

Smoking. The way to enlightenment for the Buddhist is all about making the right choices. Smoking destroys health and so is clearly the wrong choice for a person to make.

Alcohol. The Five Precepts are rules that are accepted by Buddhists throughout their lives. As the Fifth Precept makes clear *(see quotation)*, Buddhists are expected to refrain from drugs and alcoholic drinks. Buddhism emphasises the need for each person to be alert in body and mind so that they can meditate properly.

Drug-taking. Taking drugs for medicinal reasons is allowed, but the recreational abuse of drugs is not. They impede people in their search for enlightenment. They destroy a person's health. Spending money on drugs is a total waste. Buddhists are not allowed to do anything that impairs their own health or that of others.

IMPORTANT WORDS

Five Precepts; rules binding on monks and lay Buddhists to avoid killing, theft, luxury, falsehood and alcohol and drugs

IT'S A FACT

The Sigalovada Sutta in the Pali Canon of Buddhism lists six dangers of addiction to intoxicating substances:

1. loss of wealth – addiction is costly
2. increase of quarrels – such substances can make a person argumentative
3. susceptibility to disease – prolonged addiction destroys a person's health
4. loss of good character – a person known as an addict loses the respect of other people
5. indecent exposure – addictions causes a person to lose their inhibitions and act immorally
6. impaired intelligence – substances affect the brain and the ability to think clearly.

Tasks

1. What is the Hindu attitude to:
   a. smoking   b. alcohol
   c. drug-taking?
2. Why are Sikhs opposed to the drinking of alcohol?
3. Give **THREE** reasons why Buddhists are opposed to the drinking of alcohol and the taking of drugs.

SUMMARY

1 Many Hindus smoke and drink. Although Hinduism condemns drug-taking, drugs are taken by some holy men.

2 Sikhism does not allow Khalsa members to smoke or drink. Drugs are also not allowed, although many people took drugs in the time of Guru Nanak.

3 Buddhists are encouraged to abstain from smoking, drinking alcohol and taking drugs – they cloud the mind and make meditation impossible.

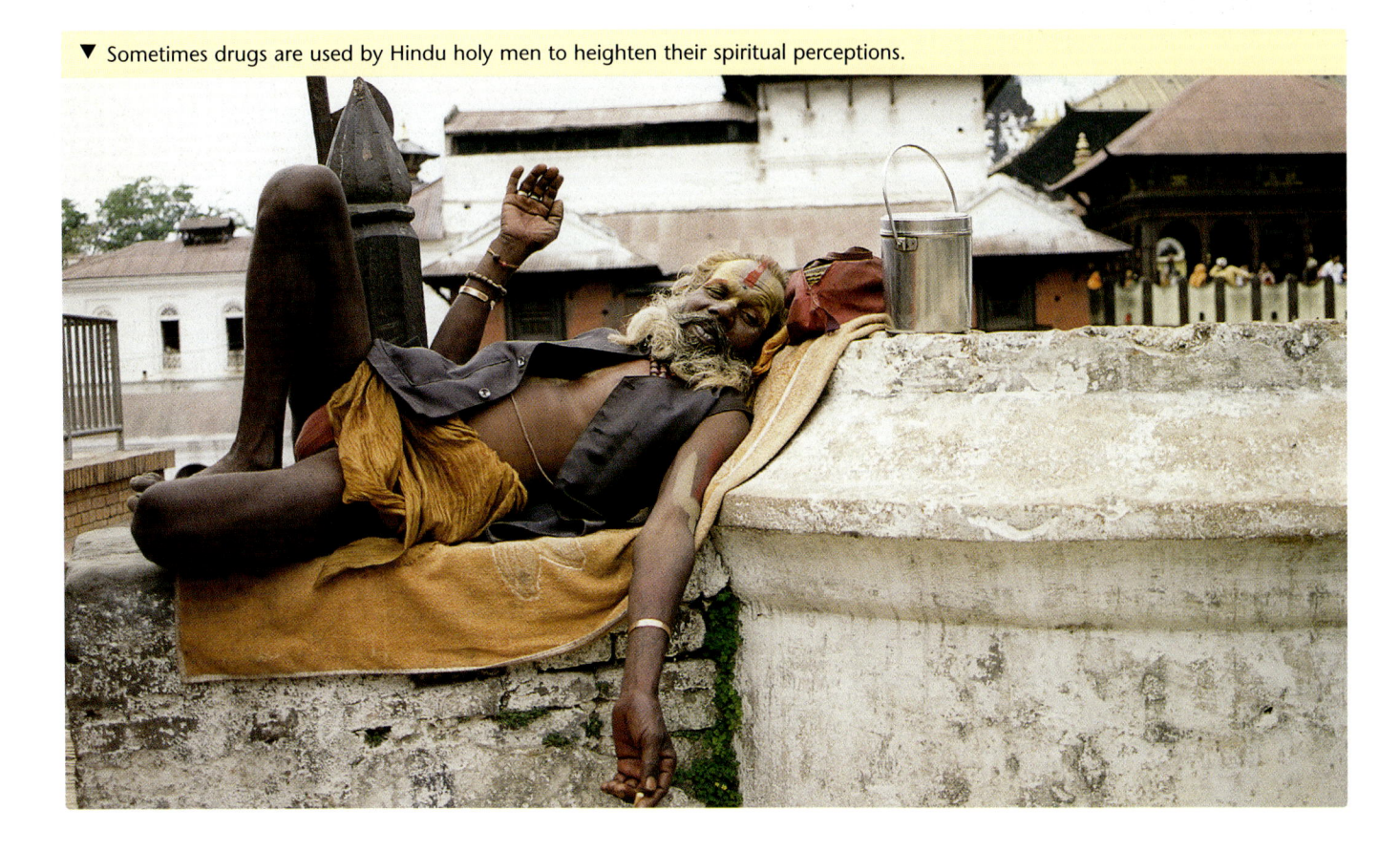

▼ Sometimes drugs are used by Hindu holy men to heighten their spiritual perceptions.

83

DRUG ABUSE

✓ Exam help ...

Most people agree that illegal drug-taking is one of the most serious problems facing modern society. A drug is a substance (medicinal, narcotic or stimulant) that has a chemical effect on the body. Even the taking of legal drugs must be supervised. You need to be aware of the reasons why many people take drugs illegally. You must also understand why the link between drugs and sport is considered to be important. There are three categories of drugs, Class A, Class B and Class C, and different dangers are associated with each of them. You will need to show that you understand that alcohol and nicotine are also drugs which can have serious side-effects.

1.a. What is a drug?
b. Why do people take drugs?

1.a. A drug is any substance that, when taken into the body, alters its chemical state/there are legal drugs that are widely used, such as alcohol and tobacco/because they are legal does not mean that they are safe. Illegal drugs such as cocaine and heroin are much more dangerous in themselves, but used by far fewer people. Both legal and illegal drugs are called 'recreational' drugs.

b. Recreational drugs are taken for a variety of reasons – to escape boredom/to experiment/to demonstrate rebellion/to find out what it feels like/the pressure of friends/because they are addicted.

2. What do the major world religions teach about the taking of drugs?

2. The major world religions draw a line between the medicinal and the recreational use of drugs. The former is supported and the latter is condemned.

Christianity: medically directed drugs are part of God's good creation/some Christians opposed to drinking of alcohol/majority support its consumption in moderation/Jesus came to help people in need/drug-takers are in desperate need/Christians involved in work of drug rehabilitation.

continued ...

Judaism: alcohol plays an important part in Jewish religious ceremonies and some festivals/teaching that the mind should always be clear, Purim festival is an exception/drug-taking opposed.

Islam: alcohol is forbidden in Islam/illegal drugs against spirit of Islam/pains and problems of life must be accepted and faced – they are the will of Allah to test the faith of each person.

Hinduism: both smoking and alcohol are tolerated/many Hindus condemn taking of drugs/some holy men take drugs as part of their devotion/addiction to be avoided.

Sikhism: the body is a temple built by God/body should be respected/all illegal use of drugs plus alcohol can ruin the health of the body/mind should always be kept free of outside influences and control.

Buddhism: the Fifth Precept – avoiding drugs and alcohol – they cloud the mind and make meditation impossible/drugs are a retreat from the truth.

3. Why is the use of drugs in sport a very serious issue?

3. The use of drugs in sport is not a modern problem – it goes back to the Greeks and Romans/bribing and cheating were considered to be normal. Now most people see taking drugs in sport to be cheating/this makes it unacceptable to the sporting authorities/testing for drugs is not easy or always effective/there are ways of 'masking' the presence of many drugs in the body/sometimes taking illegal substances can cause serious health problems, even death/taking drugs can bring about serious mood changes/one problem is that the body sometimes produces similar substances naturally/sport should be a fair competition between athletes and drugs stop this/many athletes are role-models for young people – they can have a very good or bad effect on those who look up to them.

CHAPTER 5
Media and technology

The term 'media' covers all forms of communication involving both written and transmitted or oral forms. At one end of the scale are the traditional means of communication like books and newspapers. At the other end of the scale are the newer forms of communication ranging from television to the Internet. Owing to the worldwide penetration of these means of communication, those people involved in transmitting the information have become extremely powerful. Whether one is looking to the media for information, education or entertainment they have tremendous power to influence people. Because of their power there is great concern over whether the media should be controlled and, if so, how and by whom. The interest of the world religions in the media largely revolves around two contrasting points.

1. The media can be immensely useful to the world religions.

In the UK, the Christian religion has privileged access to the media of radio and television. Virtually all of the religious services broadcast are Christian although, from time to time, documentaries present information about the other world faiths. A series of talks during the Christian festival of Lent in spring 2002 on BBC Radio 4 included speakers from five religions explaining what they believed that Jesus had contributed to the world's religious understanding. In addition, all religions have access to the Internet and there are many websites devoted both to religions and to interest groups within the different world faiths. The very rapid expansion of the radio network has opened the door for religious groups to broadcast their own programmes. As the reach of such programmes is limited, so areas that have a high concentration of a particular faith can broadcast programmes for that faith, and its members, alone.

2. The media can be threatening to the world religions.

There are areas where the religions feel particularly vulnerable. A programme, for instance, on abortion or euthanasia might challenge some deeply held religious beliefs. The Christian religion in England and Wales is also safeguarded by the law on blasphemy, although this is rarely used. Other religions do not have the same protection. Great care is taken, however, to avoid broadcasting anything that could be taken as offensive or undermining to the beliefs or teachings of any world religion. Most religions encourage their members to watch programmes that are educational or informative about issues in which religion takes a deep interest. Even soaps and comedy programmes often raise issues that have a strong moral, ethical or religious perspective.

MEDIA AND TECHNOLOGY

5:1 What are the media?

What do people mean when they speak of the media?

> *Britain's poorest households are being left behind in the digital revolution because they cannot afford access to the Internet. Figures released yesterday reveal that a 'digital divide' has opened up between the poorest households and the better off.*
>
> ... THE GUARDIAN, 11 JULY 2000

The term media (or 'mass media') refers to all forms of written communication – such as books, newspapers and magazines; and transmitted or oral communication – such as radio, television, cinema and the Internet.

The mass media

The first medium of mass communication came with the invention of the printing press in the fifteenth century. This was not developed on a large scale until the seventeenth century, but as the majority of people could neither read or write it only assumed importance during the twentieth century. It was during this century that a large growth in the media took place with the beginning of BBC radio (1926), talking films (1920s), BBC television (1936), commercial television (1955), commercial radio (1972), cable television and satellite broadcasting (1985) and the widespread growth in the 1990s of personal computers with access to the Internet.

In the last 20 years there have been great changes in broadcasting and printing, brought about mainly by new technology.

- **Broadcasting.** Cable, satellite and digital broadcasting now make it possible for many more stations to go on the air. One result of this is to increase the competition for advertising, which means there is a temptation for broadcasters to go for the most popular, but not necessarily the best, programmes. This has led to the frequent accusation against broadcasters of 'dumbing down'. Digital TV now allows TV sets to become interactive, with viewers responding to information from the broadcaster. 99 per cent of UK homes now have a television set and by 2010 the majority of them will be digital.

- **Video and DVD.** Although many more people are watching films on video and DVD this has not led to lower attendance at cinemas – the reverse, in fact. Over 140 million people in the UK visit a cinema each year. 85 per cent of UK homes have a video or DVD player.

- **Print.** The developments in information technology allow newspapers and books to be produced by fewer staff, at lower costs and in a shorter time. The result has been an explosion of publications with more books, magazines and newspapers published today than ever before. The three most popular UK daily newspapers sell over 2 million copies each day. Over 10 million newspapers are now sold each day.

- **The Internet.** This has been the largest growth area in the mass media since the late 1990s. The Internet offers access to a huge range of sites and information. Many companies now offer services directly to the customer, such as booking train and theatre tickets. Most Churches and religions, as well as many individual churches, have their own website. About 25 per cent of homes now have access to the Internet whilst over 50 per cent have personal computers. Shopping on the Internet has been quite slow to catch on.

> *There is a growing belief that 'dot coms' are the future of the economy. But if you don't have access to the skills and the knowledge to thrive in that economy because of where you live, or how much money you earn, you won't be included.*
>
> ... CLAIRE SHEARMAN, COMMUNITIES ONLINE

IT'S A FACT

One of the first films ever made showed a train coming into a station. The people watching the film could not understand what was happening. Several people were injured when the crowd made a mad rush for the exit to avoid being run over by the train!

▲ The Internet has led to a great expansion of communication facilities.

Tasks

1. Explain what you understand by the term 'mass media'.
2. Write about **THREE** parts of the mass media.
3. The two quotations on page 86 suggest there is a major problem facing new developments in mass media. What is that problem?

SUMMARY

1) The term mass media refers to all forms of written and transmitted communication. These had become very sophisticated by the end of the twentieth century.

2) The digital revolution has made information readily available to most people – but the poorest are likely to lose out.

MEDIA AND TECHNOLOGY

5:2 The effects of the media

What impact do the media have on the way that people behave?

Every society needs order and predictability. This involves persuading people to behave in a way that is acceptable to others. Everyone worries when accepted standards of behaviour begin to break down. For most of us, the media are the main source of our information about the world in which we live. They inform us and educate us but also influence us. As we watch TV, read newspapers and magazines, listen to CDs, play computer games or listen to the radio we see how our role models behave. They play a very important part in determining how we behave and what we think.

The media can also prompt alternative values and ways of behaving. They highlight changes in the values of society. Take just one simple example: 20 years ago, pornographic magazines were displayed prominently in most newspaper shops. Today, due to newsagents abiding by the voluntary Code of Practice, they are stacked on the top shelf beyond the reach of children. We have realised the impact that such magazines can have on children and have decided to take steps to protect youngsters. It is also recognised that many women find these magazines degrading.

The impact of the media

It is not easy to decide just how watching television, seeing a film at the cinema, reading a book or glancing at a newspaper or magazine will affect a person. The advertising industry, however, operates on the basis that most people are open to persuasion in many different ways. It is estimated that the majority of us see more than 1000 adverts in the course of a normal week as we travel to work, go shopping or sit in the dentist's waiting room. Each advert tries to persuade us to change our normal behaviour.

We are influenced by what we see and hear in different ways.

1. **Directly.** Sometimes we will be directly influenced by what we see. Films are classified to prevent children from seeing things that are unsuitable for their age. We have a 'watershed' time on television to prevent unsuitable programmes being shown before 9pm. This is because we know that violence and sex, portrayed graphically, can have a harmful effect on those watching. Although it is true that older people can be adversely affected by what they see and hear, the younger the person, the greater the impact is likely to be. In the main, the media act responsibly and there are relatively few public outcries over the media's activities.

2. **Through personal choice.** We choose the papers we read, the programmes we watch and the films we see. Anyone who enjoys seeing violence is likely to choose to watch a violent film. The content is received and understood in different ways by the viewer. It could be argued that a violent film is unlikely to persuade a person to commit a violent act unless they had a tendency towards violence anyway.

3. **Gradually.** The media have a long-term effect and can slowly change people. Take, for example, attitudes towards women in society. Erotic scenes in films may not lead men to go out and commit a rape. They may, however, lead men to see women as sexual objects, to be treated as less than real human beings. This may, over a period of time, affect these men's behaviour in the office, the factory or at home. This can then lead to the sexual harassment of women.

Conclusion

These comments can be applied to the most widely used of the mass media – television. The average young person watches 25 hours of television a week. What effect does this have? There are three alternative responses.

- It has little direct effect. Television is too easily ignored, talked over or switched off.
- People tend to watch the things that already appeal to them or interest them. They pass over, or filter out, information that does not find a place in their mental cupboards. The main effect of television is to confirm what people already think and believe.
- Many people believe that watching too much TV is harmful in various ways.

IT'S A FACT

Medical evidence unearthed in 1935 about the dangers of smoking was concealed by the Press at the time because tobacco companies were the biggest advertisers.

Tasks

1. How do the mass media play an important part in determining how we behave and think?
2. How are we affected by the mass media?
3. What impact might watching television have on us?

> ### ! Think about …
>
> We are bombarded with information today in a way that did not happen in the past. This has been called an 'information revolution'. What do you think are the main advantages and disadvantages of having such quick and ready access to all kinds of information?

SUMMARY

1 The media play a very important part in keeping order in society. They also prompt alternative values and ways of behaving.

2 The media have different effects on people – it can be a direct effect or a gradual effect, but we exercise our personal choice in what we watch and read.

▼ The cinema staged a strong comeback in the affections of people at the end of the twentieth century. Cinema attendance in the UK hit an all time low in 1994, with only 54 million people going to see a film. In 2002, it is estimated that admissions will reach 185 million.

MEDIA AND TECHNOLOGY

5:3 Controlling the media

How are the media controlled in Britain and why is this important?

> *92 per cent of the population think that TV is too violent. Whether or not there is a market for this sort of thing is not the right question. I think the demand is a function of the supply and if we cut the supply off there will not be a demand.*
>
> ... JOHN BEYER, MEDIAWATCH-UK

The United States Constitution guarantees the right of freedom of speech and freedom of the press. All societies with democratic forms of government, as our own, believe in freedom of expression but they also have limited forms of censorship in some areas as well.

Censorship of the Press

There are two main ways in which the Press is limited in the material it can publish.

1. **The Obscene Publications Act 1964.** A newspaper, or publisher, can be prosecuted if it publishes anything that is obscene or which portrays sexual conduct in an openly offensive way. This is extremely unusual but it did happen once or twice in the 1960s.
2. **Defamation of Character – libel.** Jeffrey Archer received £500 000 from the *Daily Star* in 1987 after it accused him of having sex with a prostitute in 1989. However, Archer was jailed for perjury, relating to the 1987 case, in 2001. Newspapers run their own controlling organisation – the Press Complaints Commission – to which people can complain if they feel the Press has, for instance, unfairly invaded their privacy. It receives about 2500 complaints from the public each year.

IT'S A FACT

In 2000 the *Sunday People* wanted to print a 'kiss and tell' story about the private life of a footballer. The footballer tried to have his name kept out of the newspaper. In March 2002, a judge decided that the man's name could be published. It is very difficult to prevent the Press from publishing information as long as the story is accurate.

Censorship and television

Television has the same restrictions placed on it as the Press, but some additional ones as well. The 'watershed' is a voluntary code of practice under which the terrestrial television companies agree to show before 9pm only programmes that are suitable for family viewing. Independent television companies are also required to include nothing in their programmes that 'offends against good taste and decency'. They must not offend the followers of any religion. Adverts must not include anything illegal or dishonest. Viewers can complain directly to the BBC if they feel a programme has offended common decency or been unfairly biased. If the complaint is upheld an apology must be screened.

The National Viewers' and Listeners' Association (now known as mediawatch-uk) was set up in 1963 to campaign for greater control of the media, claiming that standards were declining sharply. Members want to protect the vulnerable, especially the young. They believe that it is worth losing some civil liberties, if necessary, to do this.

Controlling films

All films shown to the public in the UK have to be given a classification by the British Board of Film Classification (BBFC). The BBFC can order changes to be made in a film to make it suitable for showing. Local authorities are responsible for every film shown in their area and they will not allow a film to be shown that has not been passed by the Board. There are 7 film classifications in total including U (suitable for everyone) through PG (suitable for viewing with parents) and 15 (suitable for people over the age of 15) to 18 (suitable to be viewed by adults only).

It is comparatively easy to control such terrestrial media as the Press, television and films but it is far more difficult to police what is shown on the Internet. The main concern in recent years has been over child pornography. It has become illegal to download images from the Internet that it would also be illegal to obtain from any other source. It is not always possible to reach those responsible for posting such images and so the authorities concentrate on those who download them.

Most parents try to limit what their children can do on the Internet but there is real concern about 'chat rooms' where youngsters can talk to, and arrange to meet, anonymous strangers; this has obvious dangers.

▲ Lord Archer won a famous libel trial against the *Daily Star* newspaper, but was later found to have lied in court and was sent to prison.

IT'S A FACT

In 2000, mediawatch-uk says that it found 1021 scenes involving guns and 799 violent assaults in 193 films it picked at random from those shown after the watershed on terrestrial television. It also found 87 arson or bomb attacks and 36 scenes involving illegal drugs.

Tasks

1. a. What is censorship?
   b. Why might some material be censored?
2. a. How is material published in newspapers censored?
   b. Have you ever been surprised by something you have read in a newspaper? Do you think it should have been censored? Explain your answer.
3. How is censorship on television carried out?
4. Write **TWO** pieces of information about censoring the Internet.

Exam tip

Do not try to learn too many facts and figures. It is very useful, however, to be able to quote one or two to give substance to your answer.

SUMMARY

1 The media are not allowed to function without restriction.

2 Much of the censorship of the media is self-regulated although there are penalties that are sometimes imposed by outside bodies.

3 The Internet is almost impossible to regulate. Most parents try to regulate the use that their children make of the Net. Attempts are made to control those who download material on the internet rather than those who produce the material.

IMPORTANT WORDS

BBFC; British Board of Film Classification categorises films to show suitability for different age groups

Censorship; the practice of examining different forms of media and suppressing parts considered obscene or otherwise unacceptable

Watershed; the voluntary code of conduct preventing films that portray sexual and violent themes being shown before 9pm on terrestrial television

MEDIA AND TECHNOLOGY

5:4 Religious broadcasting

How does television portray and present religion in its programmes?

> *Information is power, more valuable than oil, more precious than gold. And most of it is created, stored and distributed in the rich countries.*
>
> ... **THE GAIA ATLAS OF PLANET MANAGEMENT**

The media exist to educate, inform and entertain. They also reflect what is important in the lives of those who use them and this includes religious worship.

Religious worship

For a long time religious worship has been a staple part of the diet for radio and television. The *Daily Service* is the oldest continuing programme on BBC radio having started in 1927 in the old *Home Programme*. It is still put out for 15 minutes, every weekday, on Radio 4. Another religious service is included in the schedules on Sunday mornings, together with special services during Christian festivals, such as Easter and Christmas, and special State occasions. Radio 4 also broadcasts short *Prayer for the Day* and *Thought for the Day* spots within their normal programmes. Religious worship is largely covered on television by the long-running *Songs of Praise*, although other programmes have come and gone.

These programmes are almost exclusively Christian. They provide an opportunity for people to worship in their own home if they cannot get to church. They are particularly enjoyed by the elderly, the sick and those who have young children. They are seen as an important service to the community.

Education and information

For a long time both BBC and ITV operated a 'God slot', which kept some time on Sunday free for religious programmes alone. That has long since gone. The television remains, though, a very useful medium for educating and informing its viewers about religious matters. In 2001, ITV showed the *Alpha Course* in a series of 10 hour-long programmes late on Sunday evenings. These are popular courses run to introduce people to the Christian faith. At about the same time a four-part series on the BBC, *The Son of God*, used computer-generated graphics to re-create events in the life of Jesus, especially his death and resurrection. This has since been re-screened as it proved to be very popular. Other series in recent years have looked at the world of Islam and the history of the world religions.

There are also programmes on television on a wide range of topics of interest to those who have a spiritual or religious interest in life: programmes on the environment, natural disasters such as earthquakes and floods, marriage and divorce, homosexuality, abortion and so on. These same issues, as well as being covered in newspapers and on the Internet, are also covered on Radio 4. A long-running series, *The Moral Maze*, looks at social topics from a moral perspective. Most religious people feel that it is important for them to know what is going on in the world so that they can pray about it and find ways to help those in need through their giving. Newspapers, in particular, respond to important topical issues by carrying reports and in-depth articles. The choice of a new Archbishop of Canterbury in 2002, to lead the Anglican Church worldwide, led to many articles being published.

Discussion is a very important way of interesting people in spiritual matters and issues. From time to time, programmes bring together people from different religions to discuss what unites and separates them. In the aftermath of the destruction of the World Trade Center in New York, on 11 September 2001, there were many programmes about Islam and its role in the modern world. This is one of the most important features of the mass media. They are able to respond quickly to world events, educating and informing viewers, listeners and readers.

> **IT'S A FACT**
>
> On Sunday, 3 February 2002, the following religious programmes were on radio and terrestrial television:
>
> **BBC 1** *The Heaven and Earth Show* (10am); *Songs of Praise* (5:25pm)
>
> **ITV** *My Favourite Hymns* (11am); *What's it All About?* (12:20am)
>
> **Radio 2** *Good Morning Sunday* (7am); *Sunday Half Hour* (8:30pm)
>
> **Radio 4** *Sunday* (7:10am); *Sunday Worship* (8:07am)

Televangelism

The law in the UK does not allow religious groups to bid for television licences. Radio, though, is different and there is a Christian broadcasting station, Premier Radio, operating from London. In America, the situation is

▲ The great expansion in local broadcasting has provided opportunities for religious stations and programmes.

different and evangelists are able to preach on cable and satellite television and appeal for donations to support their work. Most Christians and members of other faiths would not like to see a similar situation arise in the UK. It would allow all kinds of fringe religious groups and preachers to gain a wide audience for their message.

Tasks

1. Write a paragraph explaining how radio and television cater for those who want to use programmes to help them worship.

2. Give **TWO** examples of how television seeks to educate and inform about religion.

3. 'The media ignore the spiritual needs of people.' How far do you agree with this comment? Give reasons for your answer showing that you have considered more than one point of view. Refer to religious teachings in your answer.

SUMMARY

1. There are several programmes of Christian worship and hymn-singing on radio and television.

2. Documentaries sometimes cover topics of religious or social interest.

3. There is little in the UK media to meet the needs of those who belong to faiths other than Christianity.

4. In the UK religious groups can own their own radio stations but not television channels.

MEDIA AND TECHNOLOGY

5:5 Christianity and the media

What is the attitude of Christianity to the mass media?

Television, radio and newspapers are immensely influential. They make an immediate impact upon all of us. Visual images are the most powerful of all, such as when images are shown of child refugees in war-torn countries like Afghanistan. The various arms of the media cannot be completely neutral. The television pictures we see have to be edited; the documentary programmes have their own producers and interviewers, whilst our newspapers are owned by powerful proprietors who have their own take on the news. This is why there needs to be a variety of newspapers and radio stations and a choice of television channels to reflect a wide cross-section of political, religious and social viewpoints.

Christians and the media

Some Christians hold the media responsible, in part, for what they see as a decline in moral standards in society, in marriage and family life, in sexual behaviour and in the care extended to the needy and the outsider. The media are so powerful that when 'deviant' behaviour is portrayed on the screen many people will copy it. The Christian religion is always calling on all parts of the media to act responsibly. In the main, Christians accept, this is what happens.

The Church is particularly concerned when sensitive moral issues are portrayed on television. The 'soaps' have a very strong grip on the viewing habits of the nation and these often tackle issues such as wife-beating, abortion and racism. If portrayed well, these are important ways of educating the public. Because of the numbers watching the soaps in the UK (in excess of 14 million an episode for the most popular) thousands can be helped. Help-line information is often available after a programme that has looked at a sensitive issue. Occasionally, however, there can be a serious misjudgment of the public mood: a spoof on paedophilia on Channel 4 in 2001 was seen by many to be one such programme.

Christians and censorship

Christians have a long history of flirting with censorship. Until recently the Roman Catholic Church maintained a list of books which Catholics were instructed not to read. Even today there are Christians who would like to see a stricter control over the media. They fear that people will be corrupted by what they see, hear and read. Others, though, look on the modern media as representing enormous opportunities to spread the Christian message. Most Christian organisations have a web site that explains the work they are doing. There are also Christian radio stations. One of them, United Christian Broadcasters (UCB), offers Christian radio for the nation.

Blasphemy

The law against blasphemy is in place to protect the Christian religion in this country. It is only used very occasionally. Two successful prosecutions for blasphemy were carried out in 1922 and 1977. Blasphemy occurs when material that speaks contemptuously of God or Jesus Christ is published or broadcast. In 1977 *Gay News*, a magazine with a very small circulation, was prosecuted for publishing a poem that described the sexual feelings of a gay Roman soldier for the crucified Christ. More recently, a classification certificate was refused to the makers of *Visions of Ecstasy*, a film in which a saint, Theresa of Avila, had sexual feelings for the crucified Jesus. The law does not extend the notion of blasphemy to any religion apart from Christianity. Nor would there have been any problem with granting a certificate to *Visions of Ecstasy* if any other man, apart from Jesus, had been involved. Many people, including some Christians, feel that the law of blasphemy is now out of date.

> *The Christian faith no longer relies on the law against blasphemy, preferring to recognize that the strength of their own faith is the best armour against mockers and blasphemers.*
>
> ... **JOHN PATTEN, TORY GOVERNMENT MINISTER**

Tasks

1. a. Why does Christianity blame the media, in part, for many of the ills in society?
   b. Do you think this is fair? Give **TWO** reasons for your answer.
2. Write **TWO** sentences about the Christian attitude towards censorship.
3. a. What is blasphemy?
   b. What is distinctive about the Christian religion and the law against blasphemy?
   c. Do you think people should be restricted in what they are able to say about the Christian religion?

> **! Think about ...**
>
> Do you think that the law of blasphemy is out of date or should people still be restricted in what they write and say about the Christian religion? If there is a law against blasphemy, do you think it should be extended to cover all religions?

SUMMARY

1 Some Christians would like to see a form of censorship of the media, but others feel that they should be free.

2 The law of blasphemy only applies to the Christian religion and is rarely used.

▼ Christians recognise the enormous influence that soaps have on the majority of people. *EastEnders,* for example is watched by over 8 million viewers, rising to around 17 million when there is a particularly gripping storyline.

MEDIA AND TECHNOLOGY

5:6 Judaism and Islam, and the media

What is the attitude of Judaism and Islam to the mass media?

■ JUDAISM

> *For thirteen years I taught my tongue not to lie; for the next thirteen, I taught it to tell the truth.*
>
> **... RABBI, NINETEENTH CENTURY**

Jews believe that it is very important to be well informed about the news and current affairs. Judaism encourages people to follow the media closely. A text from the sixteenth century allows people to pass on the latest news to others, even on the Sabbath day, since such information adds to the joy of the holy day of rest. Knowing about current affairs is an enlightening experience. Even entertainment on television and elsewhere can be spiritually important since it can make people more aware of social problems and increase their compassion for those in need.

Slander and gossip

One of the greatest vices, to the Jewish way of thinking, is the passing on of slander or gossip. The Talmud puts slander in the same class as murder; a Midrash wisely comments that "even if all of slander is not believed, half of it is". Another Jewish holy book says that God will forgive human beings for all their sins – except giving another man a bad name.

These comments are clearly relevant to the mass media today. Jews feel unhappy about the way in which newspapers, for instance, delve into the private lives of those in the public spotlight. Any gossip that harms someone's reputation is strongly disapproved of. The fact that the gossip may be true is irrelevant. At the same time the mass media must be free to comment openly on important matters of the day. Jews have always maintained the right to challenge their religious and political leaders.

▼ Jews believe that they should take a very close interest in all world affairs, such as natural disasters, famine and war.

Islam

> *Be careful of excesses in promoting sale, because it may find you a market but then reduces blessing.*
>
> ... THE PROPHET MUHAMMAD, HADITH

Living in an age of high technology and mass communication, Islam is keen that its values are reflected in the media. The media are not impartial. They reflect the values that those controlling them wish to present. Some of those values conflict sharply with Muslim values. This is particularly important in such areas as marriage and the family, abortion, dress and culture, alcohol and drinking, drug-taking, homosexuality and modesty. Islam is also very concerned with the way that the Western media present the Qur'an and the standards it teaches. In Muslim countries, this is often supported by the Shariah law, which is taken directly from the Qur'an. In some Muslim countries, the media are strictly controlled so that they only present the news in a way that is compatible with the Qur'an.

Many Muslims are also particularly concerned by the way that Islamic fundamentalism, or fanaticism, is portrayed by the media. The media found it difficult to give a balanced presentation after the events of 11 September 2001. Muslim fanatics may grab the headlines, but they are not representative of the Muslim community as a whole.

Blasphemy

We have already noted that the law regarding blasphemy in this country covers Christianity, but it does not cover Islam. This meant that, in 1989, Salman Rushdie, the author of *Satanic Verses*, could not be prosecuted for blasphemy, even though many Muslims found the book deeply offensive. Instead, a fatwa (a ruling from a recognised Muslim religious authority on a point of Islamic law) was issued against the author in 1989 and is still in place. In this instance an Iranian spiritual leader issued a fatwa that placed a bounty on Salman Rushdie's head. Usually a fatwa dies with the person who pronounced it, but Iranian religious leaders have re-instated it. Most British Muslims have distanced themselves from this particular fatwa. For Muslims, a thing is blasphemous if it speaks in a derogatory way about Allah or the Prophet Muhammad.

Muslims recognise the power of advertising. They also remember the words of the Prophet Muhammad – that advertisers should be truthful and balanced when advertising their product.

IMPORTANT WORDS

Slander; a false or malicious report against someone; libel is a written form of slander, slander is a verbal attack

Shariah law; all of the commandments of God in the Qur'an

Tasks

1. Why do Jews place such an emphasis on being informed about current affairs?
2. Why are Jews unhappy with the way that the mass media often delve into the personal lives of people?
3. What is the main Muslim concern about the mass media?
4. What is the Muslim attitude to blasphemy?
5. The Jewish Talmud obviously considers slander to be one of the worst sins. Do you think this is overstating the case or is slandering a person one of the worst things we can do?

! Think about ...

Obtain a selection of religious newspapers, such as the *Jewish Chronicle* and *Islam City* or look at websites for online newspapers. Look at the types of issue being covered and discuss any similarities and differences between them. Why do you think that most religions run their own newspaper?

SUMMARY

1 Jewish people use the media freely in their desire to be well informed about events in the news. They feel very unhappy about the current preoccupation with the private lives of people. In the Jewish community slander and gossip are amongst the most serious of sins.

2 Muslims are concerned with the values that the media present. Islam is especially concerned with such areas as marriage, the family and sexual behaviour. They find anything blasphemous to be deeply offensive.

MEDIA AND TECHNOLOGY

5:7 Hinduism, Sikhism and Buddhism, and the media

What is the attitude of Hinduism, Sikhism and Buddhism to the mass media?

Hinduism

> *Non-violence, truthfulness, abstention from taking what belongs to others, purity and control of one's organs. Manu has declared these to be the sum total of the dharma (teaching).*
>
> **... THE LAWS OF MANU**

▼ Hindus have used films to re-tell many of the old Hindu legends and stories.

In Hinduism, the holy books, as highly valued as they are, do not tell the whole truth. There are no rules of the faith that apply to all Hindus in all situations. Modern media, especially films, have played a very important role in spreading information and knowledge about Hinduism, particularly its traditional stories. Bear in mind that India has a total population of over 1 billion people. Hinduism is a religion that values its traditional stories and story-telling very highly. Bollywood, located in Bombay, is as important to India as Hollywood has been to America. It produces many films that reflect Hindu values and beliefs. The two holy books, the *Mahabharata* and the *Ramayana*, have been shown on TV in the UK in recent years and have proved to be very popular. Another film featuring the Hindu goddess Santoshi Ma created a large following for this hitherto largely unknown Hindu figure.

Sikhism

Sikhism stresses the spiritual value of truthfulness in any society. Followers of Sikhism insist that the media must be used as honestly as possible to promote this ideal. Sikhs have enthusiastically embraced all parts of the media. Bhai Vir Singh was a pioneer of the mass media at the beginning of the twentieth century, arguing that as much as possible must be available in the language of the people. He founded the weekly newspaper the *News of the Khalsa* in 1899 and the paper is still published today. One of 45 demands made by the Sikhs in 1984, when they took part in an armed uprising in the Golden Temple in Amritsar, was the installation of radio transmitters so that kirtan (hymns) could be broadcast to all the people who came there to worship.

Sikhs are in a minority in the UK and well aware that the mass media could easily misrepresent them. Every attempt is made on the Internet and elsewhere to present a positive picture of the Sikh community to outsiders.

Buddhism

> *The dignity of human beings should be more important than consumer culture, which encourages people to have more and eat more than they really need.*
>
> **... A MODERN BUDDHIST**

Buddhists are enthusiastic about the media as long as it is used to ensure people are informed truthfully about the world in which they live. The media must also help people to live according to the Eightfold Path, the Four Noble Truths and the Five Precepts. If, on the other hand, the media are simply used to arouse hatred and greed in the world then Buddhists are critical of them. Many romantic magazines and television programmes encourage people to admire, and want, materialistic life-styles. They also encourage them to live sexually promiscuous lives, over-indulge in food and drink and exploit others. This goes against the whole Buddhist life-style, which encourages simplicity, generosity and kindness.

Buddhism encourages people to be critical of what they watch, listen to and read. People need to be aware of the influence that newspapers, television and radio can have on them. They need to weigh up the options before making the choices about their own life-style and those of other people around them. If they do so, people will be happier and the world will be a much better place for it. At the same time, Buddhists would oppose any form of strict censorship.

IMPORTANT WORDS

Bollywood; the film-making industry based in India
Golden Temple; the most important Sikh gurdwara, it is in Amritsar
Amritsar; the centre of Sikhism and a place of pilgrimage

Exam tip
It is not easy to distinguish between the approaches of the different religions to the media. Concentrate on one or two important points of difference with an example or two when you are trying to learn about them.

Tasks
1. Give **TWO** examples of how films are used to spread information about Hinduism.
2. Write a paragraph about the Sikh use of the mass media.
3. What is it that Buddhists expect from the mass media?

IT'S A FACT
One Hindu festival, the Kumbh Mela, is only held every 12 years and attracts about 8 million pilgrims. In 2001, it was televised each night in the UK over a three-week period. Many pilgrims were very unhappy about it being televised. They claimed that many involved in making the broadcast were drinking alcohol and eating meat as they worked – so offending traditional Hindu values.

SUMMARY

1. Hinduism uses the mass media, especially film, to spread information about the faith. Stories play a very important role in Hinduism and these are often turned into films.

2. Sikhism believes that the mass media should be used to spread truthfulness about the faith.

3. Buddhism believes that the mass media are often used to spread false illusions about life and the world. Buddhists should use all their influence to make sure that the mass media use their power responsibly.

▲ Bhuddists are concerned that television programmes promote greed and materialism.

MEDIA AND TECHNOLOGY

✓ Exam help ...

The mass media – television, radio, books and the Internet – are very important and influential in the modern world. They offer great opportunities to the world religions, and especially Christianity in the UK. Be aware of what those opportunities are and the attitudes of the different religions to the mass media. In particular, look at the role of religious broadcasting. Make sure that you can differentiate between the attitudes of the religions to such issues as censorship and the role of the media.

1. When we talk about the media what do we mean?

1. The term media refers to all kinds of written communication – newspapers, books and so on, and oral or transmitted communication – such as television and the Internet. The mass media began with the invention of the printing press/include radio and television and now include the Internet and digital television, which opens up the possibility of interactive television/computer games, video, DVD, mobile phones and so on show the potential extent of the market/many faiths have opened their own websites.

2. Why is there concern about the effect that the mass media can have on people?

2. The mass media are enormously influential/provide us with the role models that we copy/they put forward alternative ways of behaving/advertising is based on the belief that it can change the way people behave/often we watch things that reinforce our own ideas/children are particularly affected by television/the 9pm watershed is an important safeguard/the mass media also have a gradual effect on people/the main effect of television is to confirm what people already believe.

3. Why is religious broadcasting important?

3. To some extent religious broadcasting reflects the opinions of people in society – worship on TV is important for people who cannot reach a place of worship/often this takes the form of services/television also informs people about the different religions and the religious scene/sometimes television has a definite educative function such as the *Alpha Course*/television also carries programmes on social subjects that are of religious interest, such as the environment/religious discussion programmes on radio and television are important/also programmes that inform about special religious occasions and festivals.

4. How are the media controlled in the UK?

4. Belief in the freedom of speech is important in the UK/this does not mean that the press and other parts of the media are free to publish anything/the Press usually regulates itself with anything obscene and defamatory being outlawed/terrestrial television also has a voluntary code of practice with the 'watershed' of 9pm being drawn between family and 'adult' programmes/BBFC films are labelled by a classification system, which gives the public an indication of the content of each film/the Internet is very difficult to control, child pornography is a real problem, the authorities concentrate on those who download such images rather than those who put them on the Net because this is easier.

CHAPTER 6
Crime and punishment

Criminal activity is a challenge to every society and there has been a serious explosion in such activity in recent years. This has led to increasing calls for the authorities to crack down hard on those who break the law. This will lead us to discuss the important question – what does punishment set out to achieve?

The major world religions agree that punishment should be society's retribution on the criminal for breaking its laws; a deterrent to put the criminal and others off from committing the same crime again; a way of protecting society from the criminal activities of a small minority; an attempt to change and reform the criminal and compensation for those who have been wronged. If punishment fails in any of these objectives then it does not offer a hopeful way forward. This leads us to question whether we can continue to lock more and more people away for a longer time as harsher penalties are imposed.

It is important to look at the different forms of punishment that we impose in the UK in the light of what we are trying to achieve through such punishment. Are heavy fines, locking a person up in prison, tagging them or putting them on probation sensible ways of trying to achieve these objectives? Clearly, they do achieve some of them. The criminal in prison is not free to commit other crimes, yet even that may be misleading. A prisoner may be inside for a minor crime and be mixing with hardened criminals. Many enter prison without a lifetime of crime behind them and leave, having served their sentence, as determined law-breakers. The price for this change may have to be paid later.

Then there is the very serious issue of the death penalty. You will discover that this raises all kinds of moral and religious questions. In taking the life of a murderer, is the State acting any better than the person who committed the crime in the first place? Can murder ever be justified as a response to murder? Many religions are opposed to the death penalty. Islam, however, teaches that it is the only suitable response to the crime of murder. Half of the world has abolished the death penalty, whilst the other half retains and uses it. What religious and moral issues are involved here?

CRIME AND PUNISHMENT

6:1 Crime

Has there been a recent explosion in crime?

> *The recent drop in crime shows that it is not bound irremediably and irrevocably to rise. By targeting and crime prevention campaigns, we can make a difference. The message has to be that the fear of crime must now reduce. The fear of crime in many people is worse than the problem itself.*
>
> ... DAVID MACLEAN, HOME OFFICE MINISTER, DECEMBER 1995

Crime rates

Crime figures in the UK have risen steadily during the last 50 years.

- In 1951, 638 000 crimes were reported to the police; in 1971 this figure rose to 1 900 000; by 1986 it had reached 4 million and in 2002 it stands at over 7 million.

Overall recorded crime has fallen, as the number of burglaries and car thefts decrease. However, there is a rise in violent crime and robbery. The rise in robbery figures is mostly due to the stealing of mobile phones from teenagers.

- For every crime reported, at least three go unreported. People either think that what has happened to them is too trivial to report or they may be too embarrassed.
- It is thought that over 30 million crimes are committed each year in the UK. Over 30 per cent of the population suffer from crime each year. Rural areas suffer almost as badly as urban areas.
- Most crimes are committed by people under the age of 25, the majority of criminals are between the ages of 16 and 19. Burglaries, car thefts and arson attacks, carried out by 18–20-year-olds alone, cost households and businesses £4 billion a year in the UK. Men are 7 times more likely to commit a crime than women. Men commit about 6 million known crimes a year, but are thought to be responsible for at least three times this number. 1 in 16 of all houses are burgled each year. The perpetrators of about 20 per cent of all crimes, just 1 in 5, are caught and punished. In some parts of the country the detection rate is even lower.

▼ Widespread car ownership has led to an increase in car crime. Due to the advances in car alarms, criminals are turning to car-jacking (stealing a car from a driver by force).

▲ Stealing and setting cars alight have become popular activities for vandals.

Why is there so much crime?

Many reasons have been put forward to explain the increase in the number of crimes committed. Some of the explanations are purely practical reflecting changes in everyday life – there is more to steal now, everyone now has a phone to report crime. About 20 per cent of all crime involves cars – breaking and entering, stealing, speeding and drink-driving. There are also more criminal offences in the statute-book than there used to be. Questions about criminal activity have implications for the society in which we live.

- How much is unemployment, especially amongst young people, responsible for the great increase in vandalism? In 2002, unemployment was comparatively low and yet crime was increasing steadily.
- Do advertising and television stimulate greed and the desire to have what we cannot afford? Highly desirable goods are very visible and young people today are well aware of what their contemporaries own.
- If the detection rate were higher, would that act as a deterrent? Would there be less crime if the police were more visible on the streets? Would stiffer penalties cut the amount of crime? In January 2002, the Lord Chief Justice announced that anyone stealing a mobile phone could expect to go to prison for at least four years. An increasing number of phones are stolen each week – will this new strategy work?
- Does the increase in criminal activity stem from a breakdown in moral and spiritual values in society? Is human nature naturally sinful and criminal activity an inevitable expression of this? The traditional Christian belief is that human beings have a tendency towards committing evil actions from the moment they are born. Other religions blame a breakdown of standards in society on the loss in some people of a spiritual outlook on life.

Tasks

1. Give **THREE** examples of the explosion of particular crimes in the UK in recent years.
2. Write down **TWO** pieces of information about the pattern of crimes committed.
3. Take **TWO** of the questions asked in this unit and write down **TWO** possible answers.
4. Write down **THREE** reasons why you think that some people break the law.
5. Why do you think that men are more likely than woman and the young more likely than older people to break the law?

SUMMARY

1 There has been a crime explosion in the UK in recent years for particular crimes. There are at least 30 million crimes committed each year.

2 Many reasons have been put forward to explain the increase in crime, including the suggestion that it points to a spiritual and moral breakdown in our society.

CRIME AND PUNISHMENT

6:2 Punishment

What is punishing a criminal intended to achieve?

> *Do not judge others, so that God will not judge you, for God will judge you in the same way as you judge others.*
>
> **... THE BIBLE (MATTHEW 7.1)**

Punishment is the way that society makes a person pay for a crime they have committed. This payment may involve the loss of personal freedom (prison); the inconvenience of having one's freedom restricted (probation, community service or tagging) or the payment of a sum of money (a fine). This leads us to ask a very basic question – what does any punishment, whatever it is, set out to achieve? Five answers are usually given to this question.

1. **Protection.** Criminals threaten the stability of society and, in particular, they are a threat to the most vulnerable members of the community. Everyone would agree that society needs to be protected from hardened criminals. Locking people away guarantees that society is safe from them whilst they are in prison. Most people see this as the main reason for passing a prison sentence. However, it has been argued that during a prison sentence prisoners are mixing with other criminals and so this may reinforce tendencies to break the law.

2. **Retribution.** This means making a person pay for the crime they have committed. The criminal owes society a debt – the more serious the crime the greater the debt. The problem lies in deciding which punishment is appropriate for the crime. This becomes particularly difficult when we look at capital punishment. Whatever the punishment, the criminal is paying the debt that society has decided is appropriate.

3. **Deterrence.** Each punishment is intended to deter someone who has committed a crime from doing the same thing again. It is also intended to remind other people what they can expect to receive if they commit the same crime. Opinion is divided as to how effective punishment is as a deterrent. Over 80 per cent of criminals are 'recidivists', that is they offend more than once. Many criminals return to prison time and time again after committing the same, or similar, offences. Capital punishment (the death penalty) is the 'ultimate deterrent' yet, since it was reintroduced and stepped-up in 1976 in the USA, there is still a large number of murders. If it is used there simply as a deterrent it is a failure.

▼ The number of inmates in UK prisons has exploded in recent years.

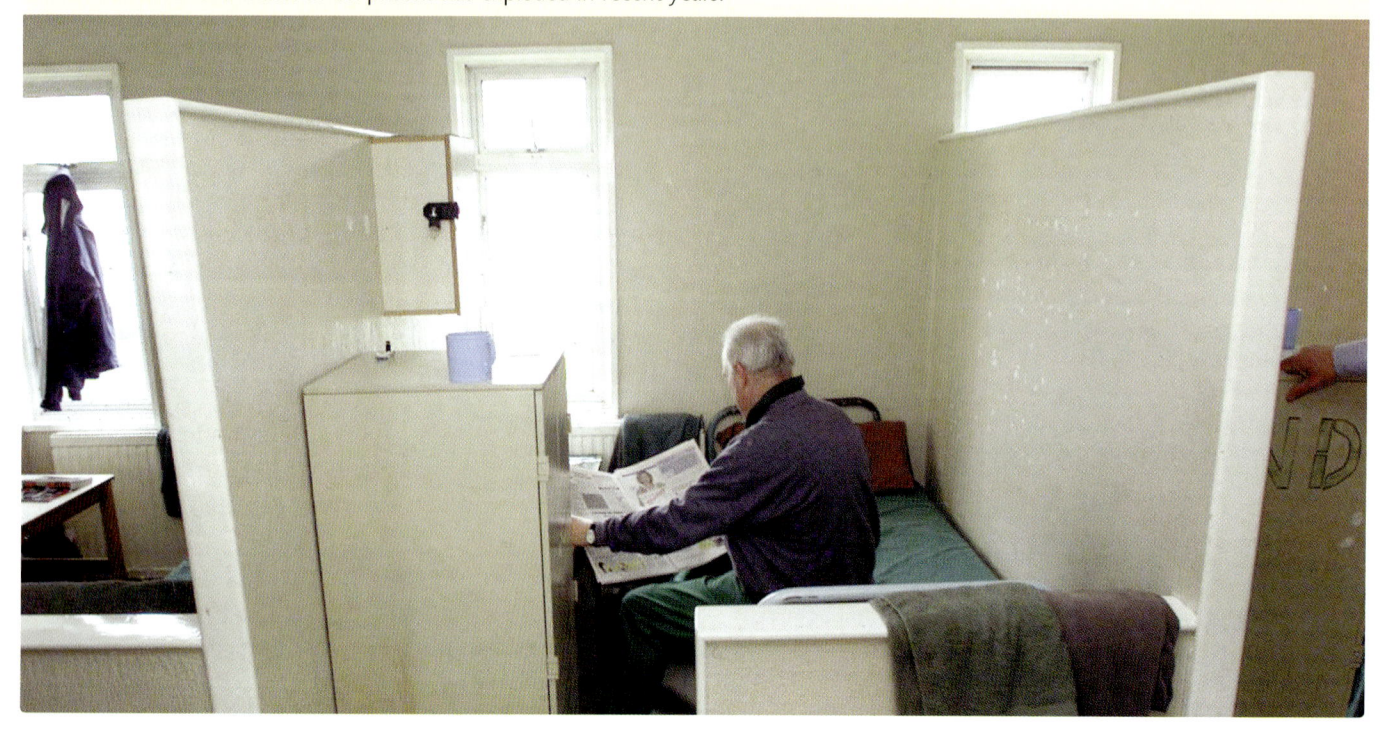

▲ Some people blame the lack of police on the street for the increase in crime.

4. **Reformation.** Whilst a person is locked away it is very important to make an attempt to reform him or her – to change their ways. Over 200 000 young people pass through the juvenile courts each year and it is crucial that an attempt is made to reform them before they become hardened criminals. In some prisons, attempts are made to educate prisoners, teach them a trade, find them somewhere to live when they are released and arrange a job for them. At the same time sessions are held to help them to see the effect their crime has had on their victims. Prisons, though, are severely overcrowded and this makes it very difficult, and often impossible, to carry out effective reformative work.

5. **Vindication.** Few of us would enjoy living in a lawless society in which chaos reigned. If people break the law, they must understand what they are doing and the punishments that are used to vindicate (justify) the law.

> *You have heard that it was said, 'An eye for an eye and a tooth for a tooth'. But now I tell you: do not take revenge on someone who wrongs you. If anyone slaps you on the right cheek, let him slap your left cheek too.*
>
> ... THE BIBLE (MATTHEW 5.38–39)

❗ Think about ...

Do you think that criminals should always be made to help or compensate their victims as part of their punishment?

Tasks

1. What is meant by describing punishment as:
   a. retribution   b. a deterrent?
2. a. Write down **TWO** ways in which the prison system attempts to reform inmates.
   b. Why is it very important that prisons do attempt to reform prisoners?
3. Can you think of **TWO** reasons why it might be appropriate to bring a criminal and the victim together?
4. Place the five purposes of punishment in what you consider to be their order of importance. Give **TWO** reasons for the order that you have chosen.

IMPORTANT WORD

Tagging; an electronic device is fitted to someone released from prison so the authorities know where they are and what they are doing

SUMMARY

① Punishment is the way that society makes a criminal pay for their actions.

② Punishment has five purposes: to protect society; to exact a penalty; to deter; to reform the prisoner; to enforce vindication.

CRIME AND PUNISHMENT

6:3 Ways of punishing

How are criminals punished in the UK?

> *No one shall be subjected to torture or to cruel, inhuman or degrading treatment or punishment.*
>
> **... UNITED NATIONS UNIVERSAL DECLARATION OF HUMAN RIGHTS**

In the UK if a person breaks the law there are several forms of punishment.

1. **Imprisonment.** Each year thousands of people are sent to prison. The existing prisons in Britain were built to take no more than 35 000 prisoners. By March 2002 the number of people in prison was 73 000 and rising. Prisoners are divided into four categories:

   - **Category A** – high security prisons are for dangerous offenders that are usually escorted everywhere by two prison officers. Category A prisons are homes for terrorists and people in the first months of a life sentence while they are assessed.
   - **Category B** – high security prison for lifers moved from Category A.
   - **Category C** – people serving up to about four years; prisoners are allowed to work and mix with other inmates.
   - **Category D** – open prisons, for first-time offenders and those about to be released; there are no high surrounding walls but prisoners are kept under surveillance.
   - **Young offenders institutions** – there are over 6 000 young people in these institutions at any one time.

   The number of ex-prisoners who re-offend is very high – over 3 out of every 4. One reason for this is that prisons are so overcrowded that very little reformative work can be carried out.

2. **Fines.** A fine often accompanies another, lesser, punishment.
3. **Community service.** For less serious crimes, a person can be sentenced to do work in the community. The maximum number of hours that can be given is 240 and the minimum is 40.
4. **Suspended sentence.** This is a sentence that is delayed to see whether the person offends again. If they do re-offend, the original sentence is carried out together with any penalty for the new offence. If they do not commit another crime, the original sentence is quashed.
5. **Probation.** Under a probation sentence, those who offend have to see a probation officer for a period of time, usually between one and three years. Someone on probation cannot leave the area without obtaining the permission of their probation officer. If they break the terms of their probation order they find themselves back in court. A probation order can be combined with a community service order.
6. **Absolute and conditional discharges.** An 'absolute discharge' is when a person is free to leave the court without any conditions of release being imposed on them. A 'conditional discharge' takes place when a person has to promise not to re-offend. These sentences are given for minor offences.
7. **Care orders.** These are made when a criminal under the age of 18 is taken into the care of the local authority and away from their own home.
8. **Cautioning.** Some offenders, especially young people, are given a caution by the police. They are not taken before a court, but if they re-offend the caution is taken into account.
9. **Tagging.** Tagging is a new form of punishment. Electronic tags are attached to criminals who can then go about their normal business. They do not need to be in prison because the authorities always know where they are and what they are doing.

The UK has not had the death penalty for murder since 1969, although some other countries still use it. Torture, corporal punishment (caning, for example) and physical mutilation are all illegal in the UK, but used in other countries.

Parole

The majority of prisoners do not serve the full sentence that is imposed on them. They come before a Parole Board, which has to decide whether they would be a threat to the public if they were to be released before completing their sentence. Their behaviour and co-operation whilst in prison are taken into account in the final decision. This is known as 'early release' and is seen by many people as a way of easing the pressure on the prison system.

> **IT'S A FACT**
>
> Each year an average of 50 people in prison kill themselves (1 a week), whilst a further 5000 injure themselves, usually in an attempt to commit suicide.

Tasks

1. Describe, in your own words, **THREE** methods that are used in this country to punish those who break the law.
2. What do you think the Parole Board takes into account when it considers a prisoner for early release from prison?
3. It costs about £500 a week to keep someone in prison. Do you think that this is money well spent? Give at least **TWO** reasons for your answer.
4. Can you think of **TWO** advantages that tagging a person would have over sending them to prison?

SUMMARY

1 People who commit serious crimes are sent to prison. Other forms of punishment used in the UK include fines, community service, probation and tagging.

2 Some forms of punishment are more effective than others.

3 Although a major motive for punishment is the reformation of the criminal, comparatively little of this work is done.

▼ Courts are now being set up so that young people who break the law can be tried within hours of being caught. Courts are opening from early morning until late at night to get trials dealt with more quickly

CRIME AND PUNISHMENT

6:4 Capital punishment – the facts

What are the facts about capital punishment?

> "You shall not take vengeance or bear a grudge against your countrymen"
>
> ... **THE TORAH (LEVITICUS 19.18)**

> The death penalty is irrevocable – it sends innocent people to their deaths. It is a particularly cruel, calculated and cold-blooded form of killing. It does nothing to prevent violent crime. It is a violation of the right to live.
>
> ... **AMNESTY INTERNATIONAL**

The death penalty in the UK

The practice of putting people to death for killing someone or committing some other very serious crime is not new. The Romans, for example, crucified murderers and those found guilty of treason if they were not Roman citizens and beheaded those who were.

In eighteenth-century England, there were over 200 crimes punishable by death including stealing a loaf of bread and taking someone's sheep! In the years that followed, there were a number of reforms and punishments became less severe. The death penalty, however, remained for most forms of murder until 1957 when Parliament restricted it to:

- killing a policeman
- killing during an armed robbery
- killing by causing an explosion
- killing more than one person.

We now know that many people were unjustly put to death. In 1950 Timothy Evans, for instance, was hanged for murdering his daughter – but he was innocent. The murder was actually committed by John Christie who shared a house with Evans. Christie was executed in 1952 for murdering seven people. Timothy was pardoned posthumously by the Queen in 1966. The last two people in the UK to be executed were put to death in 1964. A year later Parliament abolished the death penalty for a trial period of five years and in 1969 abolished it altogether. Four debates have been held in Parliament since, in 1979, 1983, 1987 and 1988, to bring back hanging. Each time, a large majority voted against it. Interestingly on each occasion this was against the wishes of some people. In 1972, a petition of 250 000 signatures was presented to Parliament calling for the return of the death penalty for 'premeditated' murder and subsequent opinion polls registered a steady 70–75 per cent in favour of its return.

Capital punishment has been abolished throughout Europe and this is now a condition for any country that applies to join the European Union. In December 1999, Turkey, for instance, lodged an application to join the EU but the application was deferred until the death penalty was abolished in Turkey. By 2002, Turkey was still outside the EU and the death penalty was still in place, although rarely used. The death penalty is still used in countries including the USA, China and in Muslim countries, which are ruled by Shariah law (law which is based on the punishments laid down in the Qur'an). In 2001, over 3048 executions were carried out in 31 different countries. Over 2400 people were executed in China alone, by a single bullet to the back of the head. Hundreds were put to death in Iraq, the Congo and Afghanistan.

Amnesty International

Amnesty International is an organisation that is in the forefront of those working for a worldwide ban on capital punishment. To support their case, Amnesty International compiles statistics on people who are put to death throughout the world. This is because countries, such as China, try to keep their executions secret. Amnesty International also hires lawyers to defend those on trial for their life.

IT'S A FACT

By 2002:

- 74 countries had abolished the death penalty altogether.
- 15 had retained the death penalty only for exceptional crimes, such as wartime offences and treason.
- 22 countries had the death penalty, but had not carried out any executions for more than 10 years.
- 84 countries retained and used the death penalty.

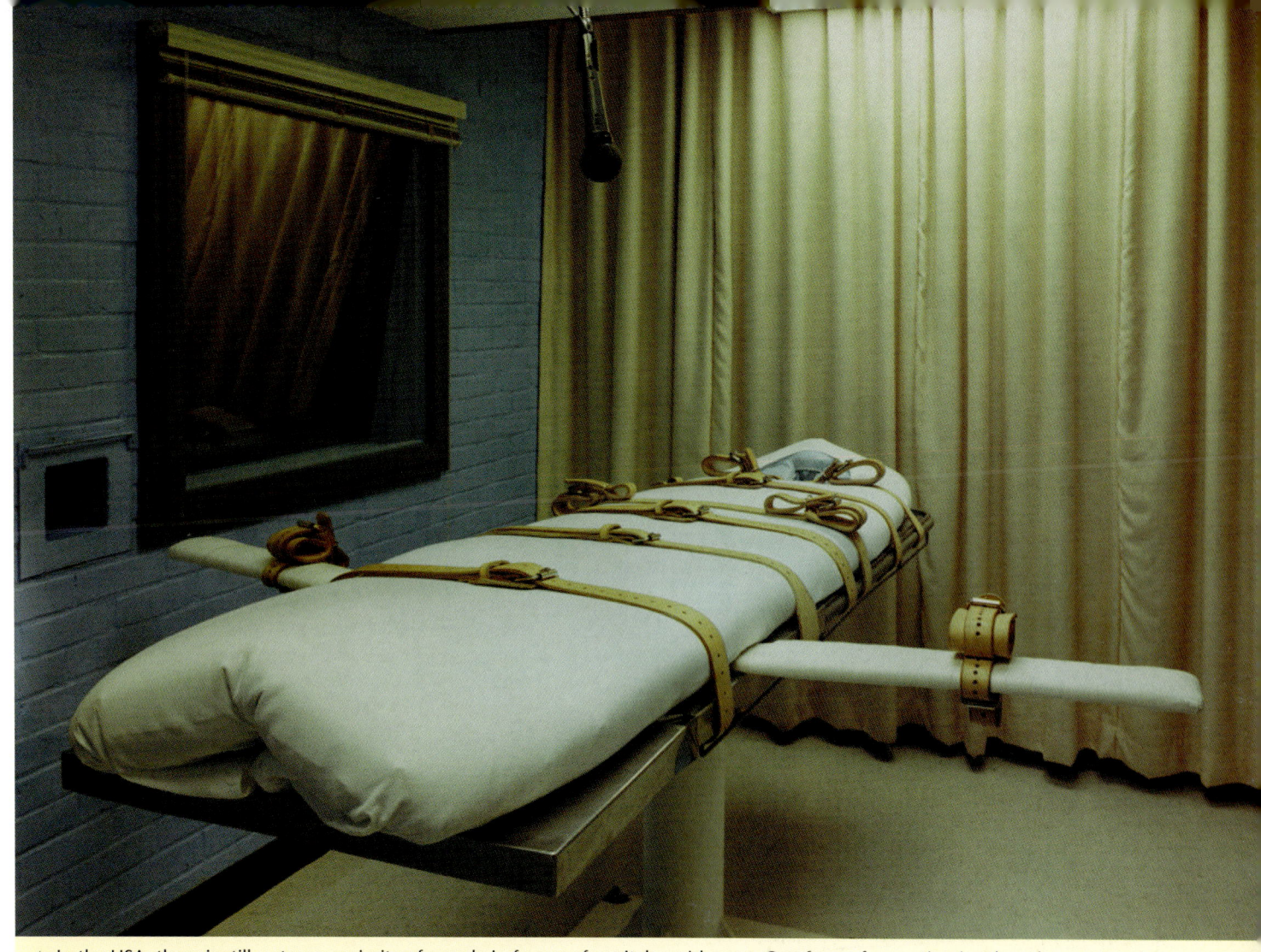

▲ In the USA, there is still a strong majority of people in favour of capital punishment. One form of execution involves the convicted person being strapped to a 'bed' and a fatal mix of chemicals being injected into their arm.

! Think about ...

The vast majority of criminals sentenced to be executed in the USA, spend more than 10 years on death row. Do you think this makes capital punishment seem even more cruel?

Tasks

1. Write a paragraph about the death penalty in the UK and the events leading up to its abolition.
2. Name **THREE** countries that still have the death penalty and use it.
3. Write down **TWO** ways in which Amnesty International tries to work towards its objective of a worldwide ban on the use of the death penalty.

SUMMARY

1 The death penalty was used in Britain until its abolition in the 1960s. It is now known that some innocent people were executed. Four attempts to restore it since have failed.

2 The death penalty is still widely used in the USA, China and other countries. Just under 50 per cent of countries in the world still have the death penalty, but many of them rarely, if ever, use it. It is not used by any country in the European Union. Amnesty International seeks a worldwide ban.

CRIME AND PUNISHMENT

6:5 Capital punishment – the issues

What are the main arguments for and against the death penalty?

The argument about the death penalty seems to be over in the UK. It seems very unlikely that any future Parliament would vote for its re-introduction. In other parts of the world, however, this issue is still hotly debated. As we shall see the death penalty can be a very divisive issue for the world religions. These are the main arguments for and against the death penalty.

Arguments for the death penalty

- The death penalty is a proper form of retribution – the most appropriate penalty to be paid by someone who has taken the life of another person. Retribution is an important part of all punishment. Society has the right to require the ultimate penalty to be paid by those who have committed the ultimate crime.
- Some people are so violent that they only understand the language of violence. In return, capital punishment is the only effective deterrent that society has against violent people.
- Putting a murderer to death is the only effective way of protecting society, as they will never be able to kill anyone else. Protecting society is an important function of punishment.
- Society must protect its most vulnerable members – young children and the elderly. Society must also protect those at the forefront of the battle against crime, especially police officers.
- A 'life' sentence does not really mean life. Most murderers are going to be released at some time in the future and left free to harm others. Also, putting someone in prison for the rest of their life is more cruel than executing them.
- Almost every ancient society practised the death penalty. Half of the countries in the world today still use it.

Arguments against the death penalty

- The justice system is not infallible and we now know that many innocent people have been executed unjustly.
- Only God can really judge a human being. He gave life to everyone in the beginning and only He has the right to take it away. Human beings do not have a divine right.
- There is no clear evidence that the death penalty acts as a deterrent. Scientific studies have failed to find evidence that the death penalty deters crime more effectively than life imprisonment.
- In 80 per cent of murders, the victim knew the murderer well. In the majority of these cases they belonged to the same family. Domestic murderers are highly unlikely to carry out another act of violence after they have been released.
- Executing people who kill for political reasons would turn them into martyrs and this in turn would lead to more deaths. There are always people who are willing to die for a political cause to which they are fanatically committed.
- Execution is barbaric. Life is sacred and cannot be taken in this way in a civilised society. Society is little more than a murderer itself if it executes criminals. Execution is no better than state-sponsored murder.

IT'S A FACT

Since 1973, 99 prisoners have been released from death row in the USA after evidence emerged of their innocence. Some had come close to execution after spending many years under sentence of death.

> *Innocent people have been hanged in the past and will be hanged in the future, unless the death penalty is abolished worldwide or the fallibility of human judgement is abolished and judges become superhuman.*
>
> **... ARTHUR KOESTLER, AUTHOR**

Clearly the death penalty is one of the most emotive of subjects. It is very difficult to feel any sympathy for the criminal who kills a young child or a defenceless old person. However, many people feel that the death penalty is not appropriate in a civilised society.

Tasks

1. a. What is capital punishment?

b. It has been said that capital punishment should have no place in a civilised society. Do you agree with this opinion? Give **TWO** reasons for your answer.

c. What arguments can be put forward for retaining the death penalty?

d. What arguments can be put forward for abolishing the death penalty?

2. Write a paragraph making out your own case for either abolishing or retaining the death penalty.

3. 'Execution is less degrading than keeping someone locked up in prison for life.' How far do you agree with this comment? Give reasons for your answer, showing that you have thought about more than one point of view. Refer to religious teachings in your answer.

! Think about ...

It has been said that the death penalty 'brutalises' the whole of society. What do you think this means? Do you agree with the comment?

SUMMARY

1 Although the death penalty has been abolished in the UK a majority of people seem to support it.

2 The arguments in favour of the death penalty point to the need for retribution and a deterrent against violent crime. They also emphasise the need to protect the most vulnerable members of society.

3 The arguments against the death penalty point to the possibility of executing an innocent person and the barbarity of the punishment itself. They also point out that the majority of murders are committed within the family.

▼ Amnesty International is at the forefront of those campaigning for an abolition of the death penalty.

CRIME AND PUNISHMENT

6:6 Christianity and punishment

What is the Christian approach to punishment?

> *Everyone must obey the state authorities, because no authority exists without God's permission and the existing authorities have been put there by God.*
>
> **... THE BIBLE (ROMANS 13.1)**

▼ Many Christians, such as the Reverend Jesse Jackson (shown here), were prominent in the fight against apartheid in South Africa in the 1980s.

Keeping the law – and breaking it

Christians accept that laws are for the good of society and that breaking them will lead to punishment. There are, however, occasions when Christians feel that it is necessary to break certain laws. These are laws that they consider to be unjust. This was the case, for instance, during the apartheid regime in South Africa during the 1970s and 1980s when church leaders were amongst those in the forefront of opposing laws that were unfair to black people.

Generally, though, Christians accept that the law should be upheld and people who break it should be punished. The law reassures people that they are protected. The law also tells the criminal, however, that once a punishment has been served they can begin to build a new life.

Christians insist that the law and any punishment are both fair and appropriate. Punishment can so easily be degrading and humiliating – and that is wrong. Until recently the policy of 'slopping out' was part of prison life, but this was intensely humiliating for everyone concerned. It is still practised in some prisons, most notably Dartmoor. In the past, some Christians have led the fight for the humane treatment of prisoners and the provision of better facilities. At the beginning of the nineteenth century, Elizabeth Fry, a Quaker, was one of the first to stress the need for prisoners to be given basic human rights.

Capital punishment

> *Preserving the common good of society requires rendering the aggressor unable to inflict harm. The traditional teaching of the Church has acknowledged the right and duty of legitimate public authority to punish criminals by means of penalties in keeping with the gravity of the crime, not excluding, in cases of extreme gravity, the death penalty.*
>
> **... CATECHISM OF THE CATHOLIC CHURCH, 1994**

Two views of capital punishment are expressed in the modern Christian community.

1. Most Christians are opposed to capital punishment. They see it as a direct challenge to the command of Jesus that his followers should love and respect their neighbour. The Church of England has been amongst those churches that have argued that capital punishment is not a real deterrent and that it is far

too easy to execute a person who could be innocent. It also removes the possibility of criminals repenting of their crime and other people extending genuine forgiveness to them. This is the basic principle that must underlie the Christian approach to crime and punishment – however serious the crime committed.

2. A minority support the use of capital punishment. Few Churches in the USA, for instance, actively oppose the death penalty. When the 'New Catechism of the Catholic Church' was published in 1994, many people were surprised to discover that it supported the use of the death penalty 'in cases of extreme gravity'.

Forgiveness

Jesus told Peter that his followers should forgive others unreservedly (Matthew 18.21–22). In the Lord's Prayer, Jesus taught his disciples to ask God to "... forgive us the wrongs we have done, as we forgive the wrongs that others have done to us." (Matthew 6.12) During the last few hours of his life Jesus asked that God's forgiveness might be given to the Roman soldiers who were nailing him to the cross, and to one of the criminals being crucified with him. Christians believe that the possibility of forgiveness should always remain open to the criminal, as long as he or she repents of their crime first.

> ! **Think about ...**
>
> The Church of England opposes capital punishment because it claims that it does not have a deterrent effect. Do you think the church should support it, if it could be shown that it does have a deterrent effect?

Tasks

1. Give **ONE** example of a statement in the Bible that encourages Christians to believe that they should respect and obey the law.

2. Give **ONE** example from recent times of Christians disobeying what they believed to be an unjust law.

3. What does punishment have to be, if Christians are to respect the law?

4. Give **TWO** reasons why most Christians oppose capital punishment.

SUMMARY

1 Christians support the laws of their country and punishment, unless a law can be shown to be unjust.

2 Christianity believes in forgiveness being extended to the criminal once the punishment has been served. This is one reason why the majority of Christians are opposed to the use of capital punishment.

3 Christians are divided about capital punishment, although the majority of them are opposed to it.

▼ The Reverend Leroy Hebert and his wife Cecila pray with prison inmate Ray Washon. People in prison often turn to religion and ask for forgiveness.

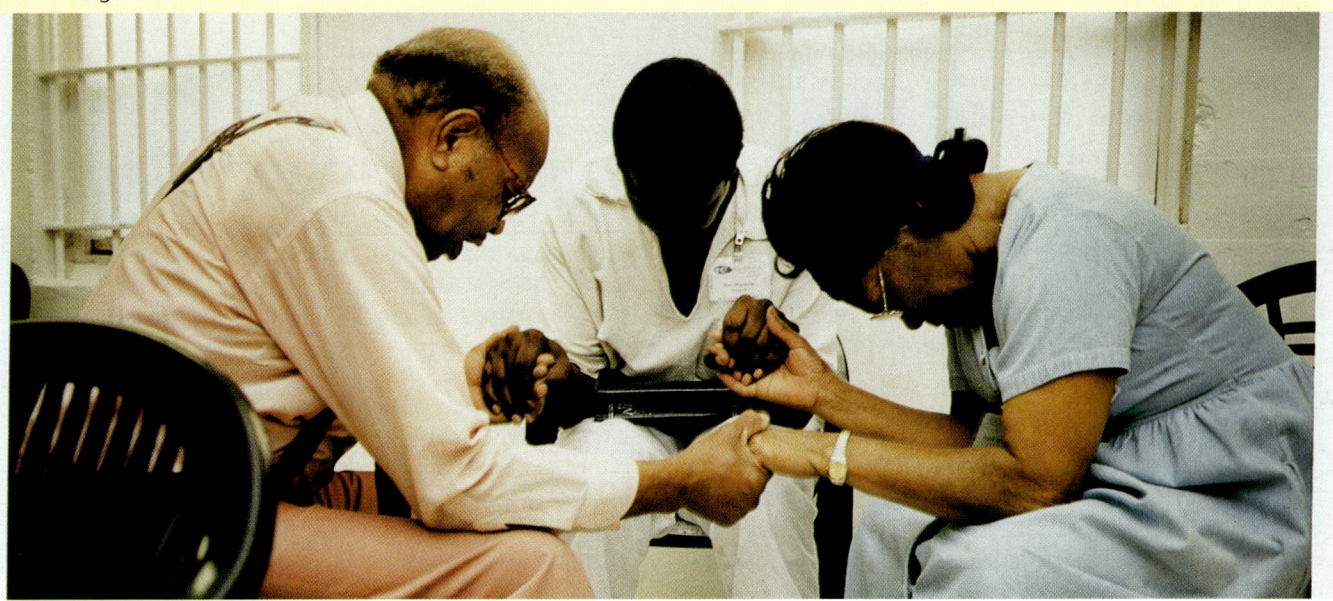

CRIME AND PUNISHMENT

6:7 Judaism and Islam, and punishment

What is the teaching of Judaism and Islam on punishment?

■ JUDAISM

> *Repentance, charity and devotion can change a grim fate.*
>
> ... **YOM KIPPUR ORDER OF SERVICE**

Until 70CE in Israel a suitable sacrifice was offered by someone who had broken the law. The sacrifices were usually of grain, oil and incense although, occasionally, an animal was offered. In that year, however, the Temple in Jerusalem was destroyed and the sacrificial system along with it. It was replaced by the 'spiritual offerings' of repentance and prayer. Nowadays, if Jews do something wrong, three courses of action are open to them.

1. **Prayer.** If a person is genuinely sorry for their actions then it is believed that their prayers will be heard by God. The prayer must include a determination by the person not to repeat the sinful action. A word of apology is not enough by itself. The repentance must be genuine and heartfelt.
2. **Charity giving.** Giving to those in need is a spiritual obligation for all Jews. It can be part of the action by a Jew to express genuinely their repentance for their actions.
3. **Fasting.** In Judaism fasting involves not eating nor drinking for a period of up to 25 hours. Fasting is a traditional religious activity for those people who wish to show their sorrow at what they have done.

The Day of Atonement

On the Day of Atonement, which falls in either September or October, a Jew makes a total reckoning of their year's behaviour along with resolutions for the coming year. All three facets of punishment play a part – the day is spent in prayer and repentance in the synagogue; fasting continues for a full 25 hours and a commitment is made to give a set amount to charity.

Capital punishment

Although the death penalty is mentioned in the Torah, it is not something that Jews would support. There is not a death penalty in Israel as there must be room left for the criminal to repent of their sins.

▼ For Jews, the most important laws – God's laws – are laid down in the Torah.

■ ISLAM

> *As to the thief, male or female, cut off his other hand; a punishment by way of an example, from Allah for their crime. And Allah is Exalted in power and wise.*
>
> ... **THE QUR'AN (5.38)**

Shariah law

Muslims believe that only Allah can forgive a person for their sin. Allah is compassionate and merciful and so He forgives when the sinner turns to Him, repents of what they have done and seeks His forgiveness. Punishment, though, comes from the society that the person has wronged. A few countries base their whole legal system on the laws that are laid down in the Qur'an – this is called 'Shariah' law. In Saudi Arabia, a part of the legal system is based on Shariah law, but the secular and religious law systems operate side by side.

The Qur'an lays out the range of punishments for a whole series of crimes. Adultery, fornication and homosexual sex are roundly condemned. Adultery, for instance, is punished by beating or stoning. Defaming a person's good name is also a serious crime. Anyone, for example, who accuses someone of adultery, needs to be able to produce four witnesses to back up their claims.

If they cannot do this they are sentenced to 80 lashes and their testimony is not believed in future.

Capital punishment

Islam recognises two crimes as being worthy of death – murder and the defamation of the names of Allah and the Prophet Muhammad. As far as murder is concerned, the nearest relative of the murdered person has the right to pardon the murderer and accept a sum of money rather than go ahead with the execution.

IT'S A FACT

The principle of 'an eye for an eye, a tooth for a tooth' is the oldest principle of Jewish justice. The Talmud, though, understands it to refer to the criminal paying money to the victim to put right what they have done. It is not a simple call for revenge.

IMPORTANT WORDS

Day of Atonement; also called 'Yom Kippur', day on which all Jews seek God's forgiveness for their sins
Jerusalem; city that is sacred to all Jews, capital of modern Israel
Shariah law; tells Muslims how to behave and prescribes penalties for lawbreaking

Tasks

1. a. What is the attitude of Judaism to capital punishment?
   b. What is the attitude of Islam to capital punishment?
2. a. What are the **THREE** things that Judaism expects from those who want to be forgiven for any sin they have committed?
   b. Write a sentence about each of them, explaining why they are important.
3. Explain what Shariah law is and give **TWO** examples of it.

! Think about ...

Jews have a special day on which they can seek God's forgiveness for the past and seek Divine help for the future. Do you think this is a good idea? Give **TWO** reasons for your answer.

▲ Each year, on the Day of Atonement, Jews believe their actions are weighed in the balance by God.

SUMMARY

1 Jews seek forgiveness for their sins through prayer, fasting and giving to charity.

2 In some countries the laws are based on the Qur'an – this is called Shariah law.

3 Shariah law gives Muslims a strong commitment to the death penalty for murder and defamation of the faith.

6:8 Hinduism, Sikhism and Buddhism, and punishment

What are the teachings of Hinduism, Sikhism and Buddhism on punishment?

■ HINDUISM

> *If punishment is properly inflicted after due consideration, it makes all people happy, but inflicted without due consideration it destroys everything.*
>
> ... MANUSMRITI (HINDU HOLY BOOKS 7.19)

The various Hindu holy books say different things about punishment. Punishments were originally very severe in Hindu society, but a more lenient system was introduced later. Forgers of royal documents, robbers, thieves, adulterers and those who had sex with members of the lowest caste were treated most severely and the death penalty could be imposed.

Punishment and caste

The Hindu texts agree on one thing – the caste status of the offender and the victim were important in assessing the punishment. Murderers of a Brahmin, the highest caste, committed the most serious crime. No corporal or capital punishment can be inflicted on a Brahmin. The most common punishment suggested is that the criminal should be reduced to a lower caste. Hindus believe in reincarnation and so this could be serious in the next rebirth.

Although the laws in India based on caste were outlawed in the 1940s they are still influential in forming Hindus' opinions and attitudes. Hindus in the UK do, of course, live by the laws of this country. The caste system, though, still plays an important part in everyday life for Hindus influencing such issues as the choice of marriage partner.

■ SIKHISM

Many Sikhs believe that because of the law of karma people will suffer for their evil actions in this life – or the next. Sikhs abide by two laws.

1. **The religious law.** Any Sikh who breaks the Reht Maryada (Khalsa code of conduct) – by drinking alcohol or smoking, for example – is said to be 'lapsed'. They must apologise in front of the congregation in the gurdwara and perform a penance to be reinstated. The penance is usually to carry out some form of public service in the gurdwara. The person can then be reinstated but they must take amrit (sugared water) and repeat their vows before this can happen.

2. **The civil law.** Sikhs accept the laws of the society in which they live. Sikhs do not oppose the death penalty for certain crimes. There are, though, just causes for which breaking the law is permissible, such as opposing British rule in India in the 1940s. Those who died in this cause are revered as 'martyrs'.

▼ Sikhs accept the law of the society in which they live.

■ BUDDHISM

> *There is no support for punishment in Buddhism – no cutting off of the hand that steals, no capital punishment, no stoning of a woman accused of adultery, no criminal asylums.*
>
> ... BUDDHIST SCHOLAR

Buddhist countries do have laws and punishments for crimes committed. Buddhists are divided on the issue of capital punishment. Many argue that Buddhists must be opposed to it because it goes against their belief in loving-kindness to all forms of life. For this reason capital punishment can never be supported. Others, however, argue that some kind of threat is needed to restrict the behaviour of some people. Many accept this, but believe that the threat of banishment is sufficient to make people behave properly. It is most useful if it is left on the statute book but rarely, if ever, used.

Tasks

1. Which groups of criminals were particularly singled out in Hindu society to be treated severely?
2. Explain the link in the Hindu scriptures between a person's caste and their punishment.
3. How are people treated in the Sikh community if they break the religious law?
4. Explain the **TWO** different attitudes to capital punishment amongst Buddhists.

! Think about ...

A Sikh who breaks one of the religious laws, is always dealt with by the community as a whole. Why do you think this is? What effect do you think this public treatment might have on the person who is seeking forgiveness?

IMPORTANT WORDS

Brahmin; the highest caste in Hinduism; those called on to be priests in Hindu society are drawn from this caste

Caste; four divisions or groups in Indian society; a person's caste determines the work they do and the person they marry

Reht Maryada; official Sikh code of conduct

SUMMARY

1 The Hindu scriptures are strong on punishment. They stipulate that a member of the Brahmin caste must be dealt with in a different way from members of other castes.

2 Sikhs must accept the rules and discipline of the faith as well as the laws of the society in which they live.

3 Some Buddhists support the use of the death penalty in rare circumstances, but others believe that the faith teaches that all forms of life should be treated very carefully.

4 Hinduism, Sikhism and Buddhism are all faiths that believe in reincarnation, so the death penalty would have consequences for a subsequent rebirth.

▼ Buddhists believe that everyone has the potential to improve and correct themselves.

CRIME AND PUNISHMENT

✓ Exam help ...

All criminal activity threatens the values of society. Punishment is an attempt to limit the damage that criminals can do. Make sure that you understand and remember the five objectives of punishment. Also understand the limitations of each reason for punishment. Capital punishment is a very controversial aspect of punishment. Work your way carefully through the arguments for and against the use of capital punishment. Also link these arguments up with the teachings of the different religions about punishment in general and capital punishment in particular

1.a. What does any kind of punishment set out to achieve?

b. Does punishment work?

1.a. Punishment is society's response to the activities of the criminal/the many punishments open to society include attempts to restrict the freedom of the individual and to cause financial pain/retribution is society's right to punish anyone who breaks its laws/punishment also has a deterrent effect/punishment makes society feel protected/punishment tries to reform the criminal so making re-offending less likely and to offer some form of compensation to the victim.

b. Punishment can work, but the recidivist (re-offending) rate is high with about 25 per cent of serious criminals re-offending/difficult to do any real reforming work with the present overcrowded prison situation. Many people seem to be sent to prison when another punishment would be more appropriate.

2.a. What is capital punishment?

b. What is the attitude of the world religions to capital punishment?

2.a. The execution of someone who has committed a 'capital' crime/also called the 'death penalty'/carried out by electric chair, hanging, lethal injection, flogging and so on/carried out after a trial.

b. Capital punishment causes many religious problems.

Christianity: mainly opposed to capital punishment/teaches that the law should be upheld and that the law should be fair and sensible/many see capital punishment as a challenge to the teaching of Jesus/the possibility of making a mistake/punishment should always leave the door open for the criminal to seek forgiveness.

Judaism: death penalty in Torah but Jews would not generally support it/room for repentance and forgiveness must always be available.

Islam: death penalty supported for murder and defamation of name of Allah/Shariah law is based totally on the Qur'an and this allows the death penalty/closest relative can waive the death penalty for money payment.

Hinduism: allows use of death penalty in certain situations/traditionally punishment was administered according to caste.

Sikhism: religious 'crimes' dealt with by gurdwara/death penalty allowed for certain crimes/just reasons for opposing certain laws/people killed in such opposition are martyrs.

Buddhism: Buddhists divided on death penalty/some oppose it because it goes against their belief in loving-kindness being shown to all/others argue that a threat is needed to curtail the behaviour of a small minority.

Reincarnation – Hinduism, Sikhism and Buddhism believe in reincarnation/death penalty would have consequences for a subsequent rebirth.

CHAPTER 7
Rich and poor

2. The South (developing world)

The South or 'developing world' are those countries of Asia, Africa and Latin America that have a low standard of living. Developing countries are usually very poor (Sudan, Somalia, Afghanistan, Bangladesh) but some are less so (Peru, Bolivia, Colombia). Along with a lower standard of living go many health problems, including a shorter life expectancy: people in the developing world die younger.

People sometimes talk of the 'Second World' when they are referring mainly to those countries in the old Communist bloc, such as Russia, Hungary and Rumania. As far as their standard of living is concerned they fall between the developed and developing countries.

When discussing wealth we need to note an important distinction between absolute and relative poverty. People who live in absolute poverty are those who do not have the money to buy the basic necessities of life, such as food, clothing and shelter. There are millions of people who die prematurely in the world today, because they cannot afford these basic necessities. Very few in Britain in the twenty-first century live in absolute poverty. Many people, though, live in relative poverty. This means that a person is poor when their standard of living is compared with that of the average person living in the same country. It is relative poverty that we will be concentrating on in the pages to come. Many questions will come to mind.

- How is it that there is such a gap between the 'haves' and the 'have-nots' in the UK?
- Who is responsible for looking after the poor?
- Why is there such an unfair distribution of wealth?
- Why are the poor so poor?
- How do the main world religions look upon wealth and poverty?
- What contributions to the plight of the needy are made by homelessness; substandard housing and unemployment? Are these the cause of poverty or the result of poverty?
- What is the attitude of the world religions to gambling in general and the Lotto in particular? What effect does winning a large sum of money have on the people who hit the jackpot?
- What is going to happen as we move further into this century?

As far as wealth and poverty are concerned the world can be divided into two sections.

1. The North (developed world)

The North or 'developed world' consists of those countries that enjoy a high standard of living and includes North America, Western Europe and Australasia. Along with a higher standard of living, they have health benefits including a much greater life expectancy: people in the developed world live longer.

RICH AND POOR

7:1 The rich

Who are the rich?

One of the most obvious facts of life in the UK is that some people have far more possessions and wealth than others. Some people live in big houses, wear designer clothes, drive powerful cars and enjoy frequent holidays in exotic places. Others can barely scrape a simple existence. Some people have money to spare, whilst others find themselves falling further and further into the 'debt trap'. How unequal is the UK and how do the wealthy obtain their money?

How do people become wealthy?

Income is the flow of money that people obtain from their work, from the State in benefits or from their investments. The top 10 per cent of earners in the UK take about 27 per cent of all income, compared with the less than 3 per cent that is earned by the poorest 10 per cent of the population. The wealthy fall into three groups.

1. **The aristocrats.** These people have inherited wealth. They own vast tracts of land. The Duke of Westminster, for instance, owns 300 acres of some of the richest parts of London in Belgravia, Mayfair and Westminster. He owns 138 000 acres in all, throughout the UK. He is thought to be the richest person in the UK and in 2002 his wealth was estimated to be £3.5 billion. His wealth is largely inherited. Each year the *Sunday Times* lists the 1000 richest people and around 300 of the people in the list each year have inherited their fortunes.

2. **The owners of industry and commerce.** About 10 per cent of the population own large amounts of stocks and shares. Many highly paid people also receive generous share allocations as part of their contracts and very large 'golden handshakes' when they leave their employment. They are, of course, also free to sell their shares. Salaries of £300 000 a year are common in the City of London for people who are in the high-risk/high-reward occupations connected with commerce and finance. These people are often called 'fat cats' because of the greed with which they claim salaries that are much higher than other workers.

3. **Those who 'strike it rich'.** People who, through good fortune or talent, strike it rich. These include sports personalities, entertainers, winners of the Lotto and people who had one very good idea that turned out to be extremely successful and profitable. Will Young, for example, is a popstar, created by a television programme, who suddenly found he was an 'overnight' success.

The multi-million fortune of James Dyson was based on a revolutionary idea for a vacuum cleaner. On a 'good' day the winner of the Lotto can pocket five or six million pounds. In addition, there are, of course, the 'filthy rich'. The richest known person in the world is Bill Gates, the founder of Microsoft Computers in America. In 2002, his personal fortune was estimated at around £55 billion, but it is increasing substantially all the time.

Moral issues

Since the 1960s, although more and more people have become seriously rich, the distribution of wealth amongst the population has changed little. The really wealthy people in the UK are likely to be older, white and male just as they were in the 1960s. This raises important moral and religious questions.

- Is it right to pay enormous salaries and bonuses to a few whilst the majority are paid far less? Some people are paid less than £5 an hour whilst others are paid £70 000 an hour. Can that possibly be justified?
- Should more money be taken from the rich in tax and redistributed to the poor?

These are the kinds of question that concern many religious believers. This is an issue about which the holy books have much to say because wealth has always been unfairly distributed.

> **IT'S A FACT**
>
> 1 per cent of the population of the UK owns 20 per cent of the wealth – almost £400 billion. 10 per cent of the population owns over 50 per cent of the wealth.

> *It is much harder for a rich person to enter the Kingdom of God than for a camel to go through the eye of a needle.*
>
> **... THE BIBLE (MARK 10.25)**

> *Even if your riches increase, don't depend on them.*
>
> **... THE BIBLE (PSALMS 62.10)**

Tasks

1. Write down **THREE** things that we know about the wealthy in the UK.

2. a. Who are the wealthy?

   b. Has the balance of wealth changed in recent years?

3. Write down **THREE** reasons why you do or do not think that it is right that some people should be able to earn enormous salaries, whilst others are paid the minimum wage.

4. 'It is wrong for a few people to be very rich whilst so many are poor.' Do you agree with this comment? Give reasons for your answer and refer to religious teachings in your answer.

! Think about ...

Imagine that you were the Chancellor of the Exchequer. Think of **THREE** ways in which you would try to reach a more equal distribution of the wealth in this country.

SUMMARY

① The number of people who are seriously wealthy in the UK has increased considerably in recent years.

② Many people are wealthy through inherited money, many are paid very high incomes, whilst others become wealthy as sports people or entertainers, for example. Some strike it rich through the Lotto or because they have a very lucrative idea.

③ The very unequal society in which we live raises serious questions about the fairness of it all.

▲ The accommodation in which a person lives is often the clearest indication of their wealth – or poverty.

121

RICH AND POOR

7:2 The poor (1)

Who are the poor in the UK and why are they poor?

> ❝ ...all human beings are born free and equal in dignity and rights ... freedom from fear and want has been proclaimed as the highest aspiration of the common people ... to promote social progress and better standards of life in larger freedom. ❞
>
> ... UNIVERSAL DECLARATION OF HUMAN RIGHTS

There are two kinds of poverty.

1. **Absolute poverty.** This is where people lack the income to buy enough food, warmth and shelter to keep their family in a good state of health. Few people live in absolute poverty in the UK today, although millions do so in other countries.
2. **Relative poverty.** This is where people are poor compared with other people living in the same country. The standard by which this is judged changes. In the UK in the 1950s, not having a television was not a sign of poverty but today, with television being such an important part of life for most people, it might be taken as indicating poverty. Of course, some people may choose not to have a television and they are not necessarily poor. Poverty is to do with not being able to afford something essential. It is in this sense that the UK is said to have the highest level of child poverty in Europe.

> ❝ Britain has one of the worst records on childhood poverty in industrialised Europe. Nearly 20 per cent of young people – between 3 and 4 million – live in families that are below the official poverty line. ❞
>
> ... UNICEF REPORT

The poor

The most commonly used approach to decide how many people are living in poverty is to take 50 per cent of the average weekly wage as the defining line. This is the measure used by the government. In 1999, 25 per cent of the population, about 14 million people, were living in poverty by this definition and this was up by 10 per cent compared with 1979. 62 per cent of single parents with children; 35 per cent of single pensioners; 24 per cent of pensioner couples; 23 per cent of couples with children; 22 per cent of single people without children and 12 per cent of couples without children were living in relative poverty. Obviously, some of these people may move out of poverty as their situations improve, but this is unlikely to happen to older people. Most people who move out of poverty find themselves drawn back in again after a short time.

Help for the poor

The Beveridge Report, in 1942, led to the foundation of the UK welfare state. Over the years the State has accepted responsibility for many different kinds of support for its citizens, including housing benefit, child benefit, old age pensions, disability and invalidity benefit, free school meals and job-seekers benefit. The welfare state, formed in 1945, pledged to look after everyone 'from the cradle to the grave'.

With all this help for the poor, there is one serious problem. The 'poverty trap' into which many low-income families fall occurs when they get employment or are given a small rise in their earnings. This is because state benefits stop when a person reaches a certain level of income. This can mean that the actual increase in income a person receives when they start work is very low. They might even, strangely, lose money if they find a job or get a pay rise. This situation is called the 'poverty trap'. One of the biggest groups affected by this is single mothers, who need to pay for childcare if they go out to work and this can cost them almost as much as they earn.

The minimum wage

In the late 1990s the government introduced a minimum wage and this now stands at just over £4 a week. This is still argued to be quite low. This figure only applies to those over the age of 21 and does not include the self-employed.

Tasks

1. a. What is absolute poverty?
   b. What is relative poverty?
2. Which two groups of people in the UK are most likely to live in poverty?
3. Name **FOUR** kinds of benefit that are available for those living in poverty. Carry out your own research to find out how much is currently being paid for each benefit.

▲ In Kenya, these children compete with goats for scraps of food. There is an immense and unbridgeable gap between these children living in absolute poverty and those at the top of the tree.

! Think about …

Do you think that a minimum wage is a good thing or not? Give **TWO** reasons for your answer.

IMPORTANT WORDS

Absolute poverty; involves people who do not have enough money to buy the basic necessities of life such as food, shelter and warmth

Poverty trap; happens when someone on benefits gets a poorly paid job and lose their benefit, leaving them worse off than before

Relative poverty; involves people who are poor compared with the people around them

SUMMARY

1. Many people in the UK live in relative poverty, but few live in absolute poverty. Many are caught in the poverty trap and are worse off if they work than if they claim benefit.

2. There are many benefits that the poor and the elderly can claim. This enables them to have a standard of living that provides the bare necessities for a reasonable life.

3. The minimum wage sets the lowest wage that any full-time worker over the age of 21 should receive.

RICH AND POOR

7:3 The poor (2)

Which groups are likely to be amongst the poorest in the UK?

Some groups of people tend to be amongst the poorest in the UK.

Single parents

The number of single parents in the UK has grown from just over 500 000 at the beginning of the 1970s to the present figure of about 1 700 000. Over 60 per cent of these single parents live in poverty. Most single parents are women. They find themselves caught in the trap of having to live on state benefits or low part-time or casual wages because they have to look after their children and they cannot afford child care.

Single parents are more likely to be poor for two, connected, reasons.

- Women who come from poor backgrounds and live in social housing in areas of high unemployment are more likely to become single parents in the first place.
- Even if they are not poor before they have children, the problem of combining work with child care means that lone parents are likely to work part-time or combine work with state benefits – so leading to poverty.

The unemployed

> *All of us should eat and drink and enjoy what we have worked for. It is God's gift.*
>
> ... THE BIBLE (ECCLESIASTES 3.13)

About 65 per cent of people with incomes below half the average wage are not working. Over two million children live in households where no one is working. There are two kinds of unemployment.

- Long-term unemployment. The long-term unemployed are the people who have real problems. Not only is the long-term loss of an income very serious, but it also has a great effect on a person's confidence, leading to stress and depression. Amongst the long-term unemployed are the disabled and those made redundant in their 50s who cannot realistically hope to get another job.
- Short-term unemployment. This is less serious, although it may have serious effects on the person and their family at the time. It is thought that families really begin to suffer if the main bread-winner is out of work for longer than three months.

In spring 1998, 1 800 000 people were unemployed. By mid 2002, this figure had fallen but was beginning to rise again.

The homeless

> *A home is more than having a roof over one's head. Decent housing certainly means a place that is warm and dry and in reasonable repair. It also means security, privacy, sufficient space, a space where people can grow and make choices … . To believe that you have no control over one of the most basic areas of your life is to be devalued.*
>
> ... CHURCH OF ENGLAND REPORT, FAITH IN THE CITY, 1985

The Church of England report, *Faith in the City*, emphasised that people should not only have somewhere to live, but that it should be adequate to give them some control over their own lives. About 3 million people in the UK are thought to be living in inadequate housing. In 1997, 108 000 families were in 'priority' housing need and of this number 57 per cent had dependent children and over 10 000 included a pregnant woman in the house. 25 per cent were homeless because relatives were no longer willing or able to house them, whilst a further 25 per cent gave the breakdown of a relationship as the reason for them being without a home. In a majority of these cases the man was being violent.

There are thought to be a further 160 000 people living and sleeping rough on the streets of major cities. Once there, people become easy prey for alcohol and drug-related problems. This gives rise to a new set of problems.

> ✓ **Exam tip**
> Make sure that you know something about ONE major charity working within each area related to poverty. Find out about the work of Shelter, the Salvation Army, the Cyrenians or the Simon Community and their work among the homeless.

Tasks

1. Why are single mothers amongst the poorest people living in the UK?
2. Why do you think that the long-term unemployed have more problems than those who are unemployed for a short time? Describe **TWO** problems that you think they might have.
3. Write down **THREE** things that you think everyone has the right to expect in the home in which they live.

SUMMARY

1 Being a single parent often leads to poverty as it is difficult for a person looking after a child to work.

2 People who are long-term unemployed find that shortage of money is a permanent problem for the whole family.

3 Many people are homeless. Often the local authority cannot provide them with adequate accommodation and they end up in bed and breakfast establishments.

▼ There is a difference between the absolute poverty of this woman and the relative poverty of many people in the UK.

RICH AND POOR

7:4 Looking after the poor

Who should carry the burden of looking after the poor and disadvantaged in our society?

It is clear that millions of people in the UK have fallen into the poverty trap. It is also clear that the benefits they receive are just about the bare minimum that is needed to allow them to live a satisfactory life. Without a considerable amount of voluntary help and the work of many charities the situation would be much worse. Some of this help comes from religion-based charities, but the bulk comes from voluntary organisations that do not have any religious motivation.

Who should help?

Clearly there are many in society who need help of one kind or another. They slip through the social security net. Whose responsibility is it to help these people?

- **The government.** Some problems can only be tackled if the help comes from the State. It is the government's responsibility to increase old age pensions, unemployment benefit, sickness and disability payments in line with inflation.

- **Families.** Each family has a responsibility towards its own family members – whether they are unemployed, sick, homeless or elderly – and the world religions stress this. The main problem is that the families of poor people are usually poor themselves and cannot provide any material help.

- **Local community.** The law makes each local authority responsible for meeting the needs of the homeless in its own area. Some local authorities barely have a problem but others, mainly in large cities, carry an enormous burden.

- **Charities.** There are now over 200 000 registered charities in this country and more are being formed all the time. Twenty new charities come into existence each day in the UK! Most of them operate in very small and limited areas of concern. Some exist mainly to send money, goods and help overseas. Some, though, work with the poor and needy in this country. They raise money and spend time making information known amongst the general public. Many of them also mobilise volunteer help in a way that the government could never hope to do. Some run shops on the high street that sell second-hand goods to raise money. Others organise appeals or door-to-door collections.

▼ Help the Aged is one of the leading charities operating in the UK.

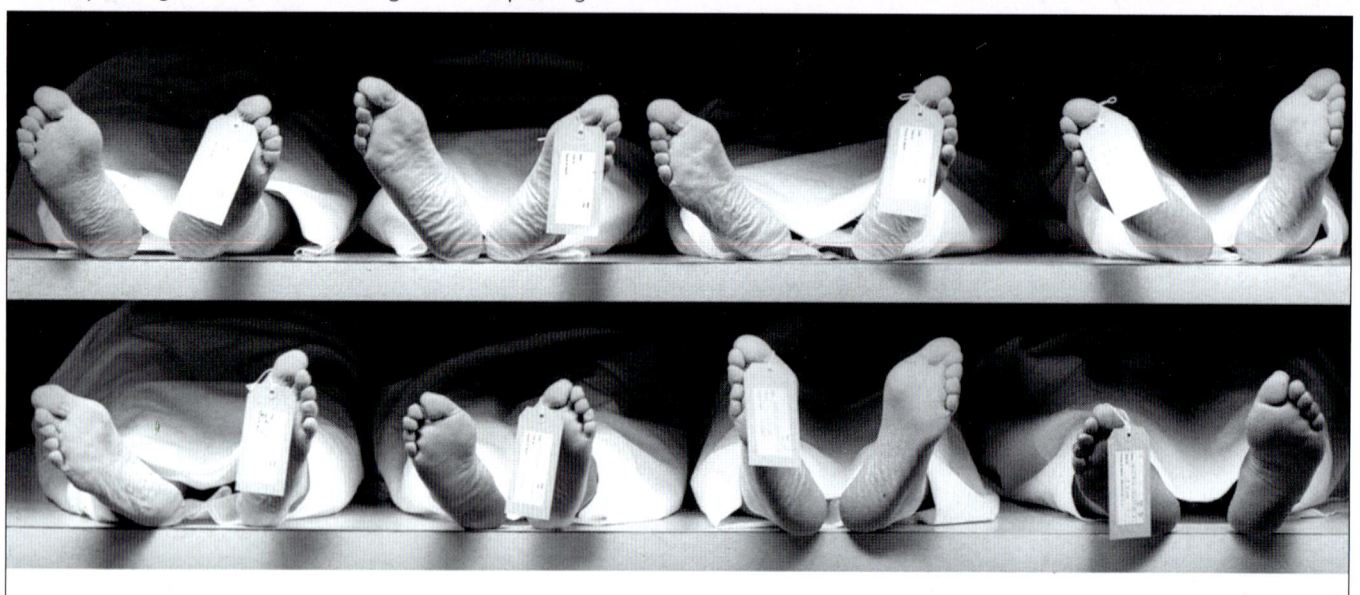

THOUSANDS OF ELDERLY PEOPLE WILL STOP FEELING THE COLD THIS WINTER

Don't let the winter kill. Call 0800 75 00 75

Help the Aged

Help the Aged

Help the Aged is one of the largest charities in the UK. This charity raises millions of pounds a year to help the elderly at home and overseas. It runs sheltered housing and day-centres for old people in cities and towns, so that good meals and company can help the elderly to avoid isolation and loneliness. It often provides buses so that the elderly can be mobile and enjoy outings.

Special efforts

During the 1980s and 1990s, special charity efforts such as Band Aid and Comic Relief were carried out nationwide to raise millions of pounds for needy causes at home and overseas. These worked by involving well-known entertainers and local groups of people in a wide variety of fund-raising efforts. Alongside these, every year the BBC runs its Children in Need appeal. In 2001 it raised over £12 million on the night of the appeal and more than £20 million overall. From these sums, grants are made throughout the year to benefit children in need at home and overseas.

IT'S A FACT

Almost 150 organisations and charities have decided to work together as the UK Coalition Against Poverty. The aim is to involve many different people, from all kinds of backgrounds, to eliminate poverty in the UK.

> *Recall the face of the poorest and the most helpless man whom you have seen, and ask yourself if the step you contemplate is going to be of any use to him.*
>
> **... WORDS OF MAHATMA GANDHI**

Tasks

1. Write about the role played by the following in helping to alleviate poverty:
   a. the government   b. families
   c. the local community.
2. Write what you think the importance of charities is.
3. Why do you think that special efforts, like Band Aid and Children in Need, have managed to raise so much money to help the poor, especially children? Find **TWO** reasons why they have proved to be so successful.

SUMMARY

1. Poverty affects many UK families. It takes efforts by government, families, charities and local authorities to fight it.

2. There are thousands of charities in the UK and many of them are fighting against poverty. Help the Aged is one of the largest charities in the UK.

3. Special efforts, like Band Aid and Children in Need, raise millions of pounds to help children at home and overseas.

▲ An elderly homeless man seeks temporary refuge in a church.

RICH AND POOR

7:5 The Lotto

What are the principles behind the Lotto and what is the money raised used for?

The Lotto

Many countries have run their own lotteries for a long time. The first National Lottery draw in the UK was held in November 1994, with a mid-week draw added three years later. In 2002, the National Lottery became the 'Lotto'. The purpose of the Lotto is two-fold.

1. To distribute large sums of money to a wide range of good causes – community efforts, arts and heritage projects, sporting facilities and charities. The largest allocation of money was paid out in 1999, to fund over 2000 projects to celebrate the new millennium. £500 million of this was allocated to a single project – the building of the Dome in Greenwich. The organisers of this project were forced to make several additional requests for money and the total grant crept upwards towards £800 million. This money was never recouped.

2. To give people the chance to win sums of money beyond their wildest dreams. Well over a thousand people have become instant millionaires with up to £6 million being paid out in a single night to individual winners.

The number of people buying lottery tickets peaked in 1999 before beginning to tail off. It had probably occurred to many would-be purchasers of tickets that odds of scooping a jackpot at 14 million to 1 were not particularly good. The organisers were so concerned about this that steps were put in place to re-launch the lottery in 2002 with more aggressive selling methods being introduced. Customers who buy other products in a shop are now to be asked at the till whether they have their lottery ticket. The terminals in shops that did not reach their 'sales targets' were to be disconnected. It remains to be seen how people will react to this.

By the beginning of 2003 well over £10 billion will have been distributed to thousands of people and thousands of good causes. It is also hoped that Britain's achievements in a variety of sports will have greatly benefited from grants made to support up-and-coming young athletes in their training. Before it was introduced, charities were very concerned that the Lotto would take money away from them. Between 1994 and 1998 their income was clearly down, but it then began to build up again.

Scratch cards

Some years after the Lotto began, instant scratch cards were introduced in shops where lottery cards could be bought. These offered 'instant' prizes and were a great success to begin with. However, real concerns were expressed that people would become addicted to them and spend more money than they could afford. It is known that people can become addicted to gambling activities that offer instant prizes. The peak of scratch cards soon passed and plans were put in place to re-launch the idea – with more imaginative ideas and larger prizes.

A moral cost?

Any form of gambling usually causes concern amongst the different religions. Islam, for instance, bans gambling in any form for its believers. Before the Lotto began, church leaders were worried about the effect that such organised gambling might have on the moral fibre of the country as a whole. These fears do not appear to have been borne out. There is little evidence that the general public has been adversely affected by the Lotto in any way.

Much of the money raised or won has improved the everyday lives of many people. There is, though, a downside. Many people have been unable to cope with the pressures of suddenly finding themselves rich beyond their wildest dreams. In 2002, a Lotto winner killed himself. He had won £2 million three years earlier, began to self-indulge and turned into a recluse. Some marriages and long-term relationships have been pushed beyond breaking point by disagreements over how the money should be divided and spent. Money, and particularly sudden wealth, does not necessarily bring happiness.

> *This is amazing – truly amazing. I have found the key that unlocks the door to eternal happiness. I will give up my job at once and simply spend, spend, spend.*
>
> **... LOTTO WINNER**

❗ Think about ...

Why do you think it can be bad for people suddenly to come into a lot of money? What do you think it might do to your family if it happened to you?

Tasks

1. What are the **TWO** reasons why the Lotto was set up in the first place?
2. List **THREE** ways in which the money raised by the Lotto is used.
3. Write **THREE** sentences about instant scratch cards.
4. Why are religious leaders concerned about the effects of the Lotto on society?

SUMMARY

1 The Lotto was introduced to distribute large sums of money to good causes and to provide the opportunity for people to win large sums of money.

▼ Since it began, the Lotto has raised and distributed millions of pounds to deserving causes.

RICH AND POOR

7:6 Christianity and wealth

What is the Christian teaching about wealth and looking after the needy?

> *What God the Father considers to be pure and genuine religion is this: to take care of orphans and widows in their suffering and to keep oneself from being corrupted by the world.*
>
> ... THE BIBLE (JAMES 1.27)

The needy

The most needy people in the modern world are those who do not have the basic necessities of life – shelter, food, clothing and a measure of personal comfort. People in the poorest countries of the world are very needy but so, too, in a different way are the poor in the richer countries. Christians are as concerned about those suffering from 'poverty of spirit' as those who are materially poor.

In responding to the needs of poor people in society Christians follow the example, and teaching, of Jesus. In the Sermon on the Mount (Matthew 5–7) Jesus reminded his followers that after performing acts of prayer and fasting they should carry out works of charity. (These were the three traditional duties of every Jew – and still are.) During his ministry Jesus showed his followers what this meant for them in practice: helping the sick, feeding the hungry, clothing the naked, caring for the disabled and others in need. He also prayed and fasted. Jesus saw his responsibility of caring for the physical and spiritual needs of others as being the two sides of the same coin.

The Christian response to the needy in the modern world is directed towards meeting the immediate needs of people and also to discovering the root cause of their needs. Both long-term and short-term projects are equally important in Christian charity. This is the message of Tear Fund, a Christian charity, which works in the neediest areas of the world.

Wealth

Christians believe that God created the world and that the whole human race should enjoy the gifts and blessings that God has provided. Money and wealth are not, in themselves, evil but they can be squandered and misused. If someone is wealthy, then it is their God-given responsibility to use their wealth for the benefit of others or else it may prevent them from entering God's kingdom – this is what Jesus told a rich young ruler who asked him how to reach eternal life (Mark 10.21). In his case, his wealth was the only thing that stopped him from becoming a disciple.

> *... the love of money is a source of all kinds of evil.*
>
> ... THE BIBLE (1 TIMOTHY 6.10)

All Christians have a duty to care for the poor and to help them with whatever means they have at their disposal. Some Christians 'tithe' by giving 10 per cent of all their income to the poor and the Church. Others take out a covenant, which involves paying a regular sum of money each month to charity. Charities can claim tax relief on this kind of giving. Many Christians also include donations to charities in their wills.

Gambling

Many Christians are very critical of gambling in any shape or form because it shows an unhealthy interest in money. They also feel that people could neglect their family if they wasted money on gambling. The only money, Christians believe that people have a right to enjoy is that which they have earned. This clearly does not include money won by gambling. Furthermore, gambling can become an addiction even when it is practised in forms like lotteries and bingo. It is recognised that there are people who are addicted to gambling. Some lose thousands of pounds through their addiction and this can have a catastrophic effect on members of their family. At the same time, it would be difficult to suggest that a pound or two spent on the lottery each week was dangerous.

> *Whoever refuses to work is not allowed to eat.*
>
> ... THE BIBLE (2 THESSALONIANS 3.10)

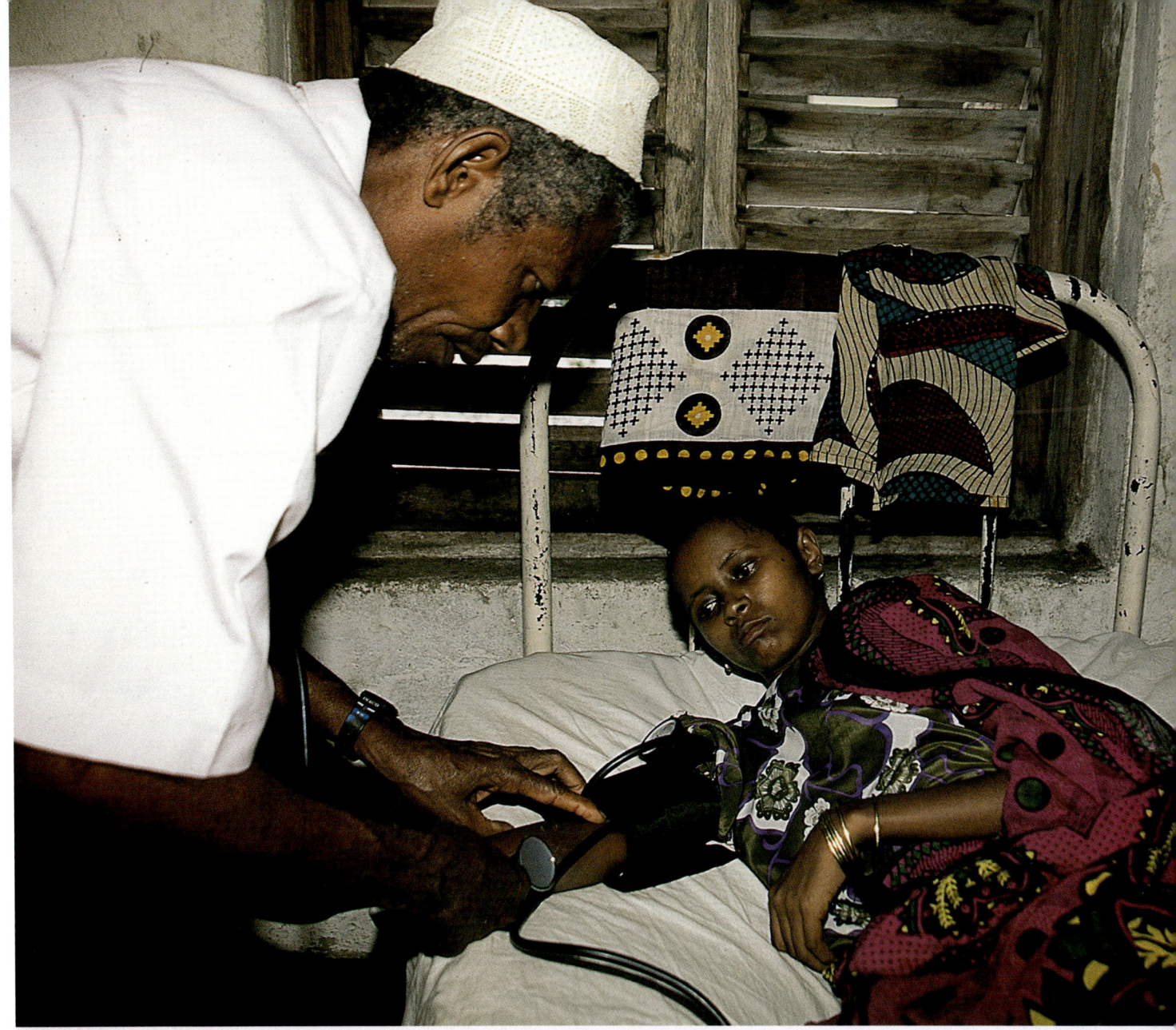

▲ Christians have a long record of working in some of the most needy parts of the world. This picture was taken in a Christian hospital in Tanzania.

Tasks

1. Look at the three quotations from the New Testament. Sum up what they have to say about money and Christian responsibility.
2. How did Jesus show Christians the way that they should treat those in need?
3. What can make wealth dangerous?
4. What is the Christian attitude towards gambling?
5. What is the main Christian duty towards other people?

SUMMARY

1 Jesus left his followers the example of how they should look after the needy in the world: they should meet their immediate needs and try to improve their situation in the long term.

2 All Christians should care for the poor. Some Christians give the traditional tithe (a tenth of their income) to help the poor.

3 Traditionally, Christianity has been strongly opposed to gambling, although most Christians do not see any danger in the Lotto.

131

RICH AND POOR

7:7 Judaism and Islam, and wealth

What do Judaism and Islam teach about wealth and poverty?

■ JUDAISM

> *Do not toil to gain wealth; have the sense to desist.*
>
> ... THE TANAKH (PROVERBS 23.4)

Wealth

There are clear warnings in the Jewish Scriptures about spending too much time and energy accumulating wealth. Judaism has always steered a middle path between striving for wealth and shunning it. Wealth is a sign of God's blessing but, if it is achieved, the person is expected to put it at the disposal of the whole community. In Jewish thought there are eight different attitudes that a person can have towards giving money to help the poor. At one end they can give less than they can afford unwillingly; that is better than nothing. At the other end of the scale they can give to the poor in such a way that the poor person's dignity is restored and they can move on to an independent existence; this is highly commendable. The worst state of all for a person to be in is not poverty but greed – greed destroys the soul.

> *Poverty is worse than fifty plagues. A poor man is reckoned as dead.*
>
> ... THE TALMUD, A JEWISH HOLY BOOK

Poverty

Within Jewish society there were four groups identified by the Scriptures as being in particular need – the fatherless, the widowed, the poor and the strangers. The fatherless and the widowed need to be cared for because they do not have a family structure to support them. The Jewish community has always loved and cared for the poor. It provided a free education for them long before this was provided by the State. The job of preparing and burying the dead, for example, is seen as the greatest of all acts of charity because the kindness cannot be repaid by the recipient.

Gambling

The Jewish holy books have little to say about gambling beyond recognising that the basic motive behind it is that of greed. Greed often leads to pride and pride stands between the worshipper and God. Jews are mainly concerned with the spiritual consequences of gambling.

■ ISLAM

Wealth

> *Riches are sweet and a source of blessing to those who acquire them by the way; but those who seek them out of greed are like people who eat but are never full.*
>
> ... THE PROPHET MUHAMMED, HADITH

Wealth is created by Allah and belongs to Him. Because Allah gives wealth to individual Muslims so He has the right to say how it should be used. Each believer should spend his wealth on himself and his family – and on those who are in need in the community.

Zakat is the way that God has provided to distribute wealth. This is one of the Five Pillars of the Faith. Each Muslim is required to give 2.5 per cent of their income each year to help, in particular, the poor and the widows in the community. This help is not to be viewed as charity – it is the right of the poor to receive it. From generous giving comes true spiritual contentment. Over and above this, Muslims are encouraged to make voluntary contributions at any time.

Poverty

Although some Muslim communities are rich due to the discovery of oil, the majority are very poor. Even poor Muslims, though, have Allah's greatest gift to enjoy – faith. Muslims everywhere deserve the support of those who can help them. Aid to the poorer parts of the Muslim world is channelled through charities, such as Islamic Relief and The Red Crescent.

Gambling

Gambling, like drinking alcohol and drug-taking, is strictly forbidden. They all lead to a loss of sense and reason and this in turn destroys faith in Allah.

IMPORTANT WORDS

Zakat; third of the Five Pillars, a religious tax payable by all Muslims to help those in need

Five Pillars; the five duties of every Muslim, including faith in Allah and making a holy pilgrimage to Makkah

Tasks

1. Look at the quote from the Talmud. What do you think it means?
2. A midrash says: 'He who has a hundred, craves for two hundred.' What do you think this holy book is warning Jews about?
3. Which ways has God provided for wealth to be re-distributed in the Muslim community?

SUMMARY

1 Jews believe that wealth is a gift from God – to be used for the benefit of the whole community. Greed is one of the worst sins. The fatherless, widowed, poor and strangers are singled out for special help.

2 Muslims believe that wealth is created by Allah and should be distributed amongst the community through zakat. It is not poverty that Muslims should fear as much as losing their faith in Allah.

3 Both Judaism and Islam recognise that it is the responsibility of all believers to tackle poverty in their communities

▼ The teaching of the Qur'an tells Muslims how they should deal with their money.

RICH AND POOR

7:8 Hinduism, Sikhism and Buddhism, and wealth

What do Hinduism, Sikhism and Buddhism teach about wealth and poverty?

■ HINDUISM

> *He who seeks happiness must strive for contentment and self-control; happiness arises from contentment, uncontrolled pursuit of wealth will result in unhappiness.*
>
> ... LAW OF MANU (4.12)

Wealth

Hindus believe that there are four basic aims in life – dharma (religious and social duty); artha (gaining wealth); kama (enjoying the good life) and moksha (freedom or liberation). Artha encourages people to earn money honestly and lawfully. Gaining money in a dishonest way taints the money and the person earning it. It will also earn them bad karma and this will affect their next rebirth – a matter of great concern to every Hindu.

Poverty

Giving to charity is an important Hindu activity but the first responsibility for looking after the needy falls on the family. Beyond this, those who are able to spare money give to the needy in their immediate area. Before their midday meal, many Hindu families give food to at least one person in need. Beggars are given money at railway stations, bus stations and outside temples. Those who give generously earn merit for the next life.

■ SIKHISM

> *Those who have money have the anxiety of greed: those without money have the anxiety of poverty.*
>
> ... ADI GRANTH, 1019

Wealth

Sikhs are realistic about wealth. All Sikhs are expected to earn honestly and share generously. They should give at least 10 per cent of their wealth away to others. Money must not be spent on pursuits such as gambling and drinking. Inheriting wealth is the result of good behaviour in a past life. Money must be honestly earned, not the result of exploiting the poor.

Poverty

Traditionally, the main concern for a Sikh was their immediate family and their village. However, as the Sikh community has become wealthier, resources have been freed for wider use. Increasingly, help is being provided for those in need well beyond the Sikh homeland of the Punjab.

■ BUDDHISM

> *Look upon the world as a bubble, look upon it as a mirage ... for the wise there is no attachment at all.*
>
> ... THE BUDDHA, DHAMMAPADA 13, 170–171

Wealth

Buddhists follow the Middle Way. This is the path between indulgence and extreme self-denial. Every human being needs enough food, clothing and shelter to be free from anxiety. However, if people have too much wealth then they might spend all of their energy guarding and increasing it. That would be a serious mistake. Attachment to wealth does not bring happiness and so must be avoided. On the 'Wheel of Life', a symbolic drawing of the suffering nature of existence, craving is illustrated by a man drinking wine. Just as a man's thirst for wine is never satisfied, so the person deluded by greed is never satisfied either and craves more and more possessions. Looking at the lives of the wealthy and famous, it is often apparent that having a lot of money does not necessarily bring happiness.

Poverty

The opposite of living in luxury is to live in such need that there is neither the time nor the energy to think about anything other than survival. Buddhism teaches that people should aim for a balance between not having

▲ The Guru Granth Sahib teaches Sikhs that their community should look after the rich and the poor equally. All people are equal in the presence of God.

enough and wanting too much. People who have too much experience the suffering of worry, meanness and craving. Those who do not have enough suffer from anxiety about survival. Neither are conducive to the growth and development of the spiritual life through meditation towards enlightenment, the true goal of every Buddhist.

Tasks

1. a. What is the teaching of Hinduism about wealth?
   b. What is the teaching of Hinduism about poverty?
2. If a Sikh is wealthy, how should their wealth be used?
3. a. What is the teaching of Buddhism about wealth?
   b. What is the teaching of Buddhism about poverty?
4. a. What is the Middle Way in Buddhism?
   b. How does the attitude of Buddhism towards wealth illustrate that it is a 'middle way'?

! Think about …

Buddhism teaches that people should try to avoid all greed and desire. Do you think this is a realistic aim?

SUMMARY

1 Becoming wealthy is one of the aims of life for a Hindu, as long as wealth is gained honestly. Giving to charity is an important Hindu duty. Looking after one's own family is the supreme responsibility.

2 Sikhs also stress the importance of earning money honestly. It must not be spent on alcohol or gambling. One's immediate family and village are the main responsibility of a Sikh.

3 Buddhism teaches the Middle Way between luxury and poverty as the ideal. Craving for wealth, or anything else, is the greatest obstacle to spiritual enlightenment.

RICH AND POOR

✓ Exam help ...

There is a great difference between those living in the richest and poorest parts of the world. In the UK the rich are mostly drawn from the aristocracy, the owners of industry and the 'suddenly rich'. Few in the UK live in absolute poverty, but there are many in relative poverty. Amongst those in relative poverty are single parents, unemployed and homeless. In the UK the poor are looked after by a combination of the government, local authorities, charities and families. Money from the Lotto is used to help a wide variety of good causes.

unemployed, the homeless, single mothers, the elderly/responsibility stressed in all religions to share wealth and look after poor/failed attempts to redistribute wealth by tax and other means/raise minimum wage/encourage people to better themselves and create their own wealth.

1. What problems might be faced by someone who suddenly finds themselves rich?

1. Sudden wealth will certainly lead to a change in lifestyle/they may have the money to give up work/work may have been very important in their lives giving them friends and companionship/these may then be lost/wealthy people may become bored/they may be tempted to spend, spend, spend/their wealth may cut them off from their friends/family and friends may expect to share in their wealth/others may give them bad advice about how to deal with their wealth/they may find it difficult to distinguish between true friends and those who want to get their hands on their wealth.

2. Why is wealth so unequally distributed in the UK and what do you think should be done about it?

2. Absolute and relative poverty/lavish lifestyle of some people – houses, cars, boats, helicopters, compared with struggling lifestyle of others/inherited wealth/compare with people in developing countries without adequate food, clean water, shelter/compare also with many people in this country who are very poor – the

continued ...

3. What do the different world religions have to say about wealth and poverty?

3. General comments – acquiring wealth should not be a preoccupation/wealth does not necessarily bring happiness/acquiring wealth can bring greed/world religions warn against greed/important to give to the poor.

Christianity: in meeting the needs of the poor Christians follow the example of Jesus – the sick, the hungry, the naked, the disabled/meeting immediate and long-term needs of the poor/wealth to be shared not squandered.

Judaism: middle path between earning wealth and squandering it/wealth given to be used for others/greed destroys/care of sick and dead seen as ultimate responsibilities.

Islam: wealth created by Allah/given to humans to be used wisely/wealth should be spent on person, family and poor in community/zakat is God-given way to distribute wealth.

Hinduism: four basic aims in life include artha (gaining of wealth)/money must be obtained honestly/next rebirth depends on honest wealth/family should look after their own and also needy in community.

Sikhism: 10 per cent given away to others/money must not be wasted/main Sikh concern for family and then the community.

Buddhism: the Middle Way between having too much and not enough/both extremes bring their own forms of pressure/attachment to wealth does not bring happiness, to be avoided/no one should need to spend whole life worrying about survival.

Truth, spirituality and contemporary issues

Glossary

A

Abortion the surgical removal of an embryo or foetus from the womb so that it is destroyed

Absolute poverty poverty which denies people the basic elements needed for human survival – clean water, food and shelter

Active euthanasia someone, other than the patient, deliberately ends the patient's life

Adultery voluntary sexual intercourse between a married person and someone who is not their partner; condemned by all world religions

Ahimsa the Hindu/Buddhist belief in non-violence, harmlessness, respect for life

AID artificial insemination by donor; implantation of sperm from an anonymous donor into a woman's uterus

AIH artificial insemination by husband; implantation of sperm from her husband into a woman's uterus

Akhand Path the continuous reading of the Guru Granth Sahib, takes 48 hours and marks special Sikh occasions

Alcohol a liquid generated by the fermentation of sugar; forming the intoxicating element of fermented liquors

Allah the supreme being worshipped by Muslims; the name for God in Islam; no images are permitted of Allah

Altar raised platform at the front of some churches where the service of Holy Communion is conducted

Amrit sugared water used at the most important Sikh ceremonies, especially initiation into the Khalsa

Amritsar sacred city of the Sikhs in the Punjab, India; home of the famous Golden Temple; founded by the fourth guru

Anglican Church the worldwide church which is based on the teachings of the Church of England

Artefact a hand-made object that can be used in worship

Artha one of the four aims in Hinduism, the acquisition of wealth

Ashram a Hindu community centred on religious teaching and spiritual living, place where a guru teaches his disciples

AUM sacred syllable in Hinduism; believed to contain basic elements of the universe

B

BBFC British Board of Film Classification

Believer's baptism practice of baptising believing adults; mainly carried out by the Baptist Church

Bhagavad Gita 'song of the blessed one', most famous and popular of the Hindu scriptures

Bible collection of scriptures sacred to the Jewish or Christian communities

Bishop highest priest in the Roman Catholic and Anglican churches

Blastocyst this forms 5–7 days after an ovum has been fertilised

Bollywood the film-making industry, based in India

Brahman the holy power believed by Hindus to be present in the whole universe; a God who is indescribable

Brahmin the highest of the castes in Hinduism; the priestly caste

Buddha the enlightened one; founder of Buddhism, Siddhartha Gautama, after his enlightenment in 531BCE

C

Caste division of classes within Hindu society; there are four castes (Brahmin – priest; Kshatriya – warrior; Vaisya – trader/farmer; Sudra – labourer) and the 'outcastes'

Capital punishment legally authorised killing of someone as punishment for a crime

Truth, spirituality and contemporary issues

Glossary continued ...

Cathedral church which contains the throne (cathedra) of the bishop; most important church in a diocese

Censorship the practice of examining different forms of media and suppressing parts considered obscene or otherwise unacceptable

Christ title given to Jesus

Christmas Christian festival which celebrates the birth of Jesus in Bethlehem

Church of England most important church in England; formed in the sixteenth century; the established church in England with privileges not given to other churches

Class A drugs most dangerous drugs including heroin, cocaine, ecstasy and LSD; possessing and selling carry heavy penalties, sometimes called 'hard' drugs

Class B drugs sometimes called 'soft' drugs, include marijuana

Cloning make an identical copy of genetic make-up to create genetically identical people or animals

Consumerism the preoccupation of society with the acquisition of consumer goods

Contraception any means which is used to prevent conception taking place during sexual intercourse

Convent building in which a female religious order lives

Crime a violation of the law, an act which is punishable by law

D

Day of Atonement (Yom Kippur), most solemn day in the Jewish year; time when Jews seek God's forgiveness so that they can remain in the book of life for another year

Day of Resurrection day when many Christians believe the dead will return to life

Dhamma another term for Dharma, among Buddhists

Dharma in Buddhism, refers to the teaching of the Buddha; one of three refuges: in Hinduism, refers to the personal duty to uphold the cosmic law

E

Easter Christian festival celebrating the death and resurrection of Jesus; starts with Good Friday and ends on Easter Sunday

Eightfold path scheme of moral and spiritual training in Buddhism designed to lead to deliverance from suffering by working through wisdom, morality and meditation; it follows on from the Four Noble Truths

Embryo fertilised ovum during the first eight weeks of pregnancy before all organs are developed

Embryo cloning removing cells from an embryo and using them to create a separate embryo

Euthanasia 'happy death'; also known as mercy killing; the assisted death of a person suffering from a terminal illness or in an irreversible coma

Everlasting light light that burns continuously in synagogues, constant reminder of the presence of God with the Jewish people

Exodus most important event in Jewish history, celebrates the journey of the Jews out of Egyptian slavery; celebrated each year during the festival of Passover

F

Five Ks symbols worn by Sikhs initiated into the khalsa – uncut hair (kesh), steel comb (kangha), shorts (kaccha), steel bangle (kara) and short sword (kirpan)

Five Pillars the five beliefs at the heart of Islam – belief in Allah (Shahadah), prayer (Salah), giving to the poor (Zakat), fasting during Ramadan (Sawm) and pilgrimage to Makkah (Hajj)

Five Precepts rules binding on monks and lay Buddhists to avoid killing, theft, luxury, falsehood and alcohol

Foetus fertilised ovum with developed organs

Four Noble Truths the set of principles by which Buddhists hope to gain enlightenment through understanding the truth about suffering

G

Gene one of the DNA responsible for passing on specific characteristics from parents to offspring

Genetic engineering a science whose aims include the control of hereditary defects by modification or elimination of certain genes

Golden Temple chief destination of Sikh pilgrims at Amritsar; built by the fifth guru beside the pool of immortality

Gospel one of four books in the New Testament which contain the life and teachings of Jesus; first three are similar and are called the synoptic (looking together) gospels

Gurdwara Sikh temple or building for worship

Guru holy man or spiritual teacher in Indian religions, especially Hinduism and Sikhism

Guru Granth Sahib the Holy Book of the Sikh religion, contains the Adi Granth and other writings; put into present form by Gobind Singh, the tenth guru

Guru Nanak the first Sikh guru (1469–1539); founder of Sikhism

H

Hajj one of the five pillars of Islam; the pilgrimage of believers to the holy city of Makkah

Haram the word for anything that is forbidden in Islam

Holy Communion central service in most churches; remembers the death and resurrection of Jesus using the symbols of bread and wine

Holy Liturgy name given in the Orthodox Church to the service of Holy Communion

Holy Spirit the third part of the Christian Trinity; given to disciples on the day of Pentecost; believed to be God's spirituality in action in the world today

Hospice a home that offers pain relief and care to those who are terminally ill

I

Icon painting or mosaic of Jesus or of Christian saints; used in the Orthodox Churches as an aid to devotion by worshippers

Illegal drug a narcotic substance, especially an addictive one

Imam man who leads public worship and prayers in a mosque

Infant baptism service in most Christian churches where a baby is baptised; traditionally seen as key to membership of the church; baptism by water

Infertile unable to reproduce

Involuntary euthanasia euthanasia when a person is physically or mentally incapable of giving their consent

Iona place of Christian pilgrimage in Scotland; St Columba built a monastery there in 563CE

IVF in vitro fertilisation, this procedure is often referred to as 'test tube baby'

J

Jehovah's Witnesses small Christian group, known for its opposition to blood transfusions

Jerusalem city which is sacred to Jews, Muslims and Christians; city outside which Jesus was crucified

K

Karma term used in Hinduism for the way in which deeds in this life determine one's destiny in reincarnation

Kashrut the Jewish dietary laws

Khalsa Sikh brotherhood, the ruling body of Sikhism, founded by Guru Gobind Singh in 1699CE

Kippah Jewish skull-cap

Kosher term applied to those categories of food which Jews are allowed by their faith to eat; also to the way in which the food is prepared

Kshatriya Hindu warrior caste

L

Langar kitchen attached to a Sikh gurdwara where the congregation enjoys a communal meal after worship

Law of double-effect applies where drugs administered to a terminally ill patient may have the side effect of hastening their death

Lord's prayer the prayer that Jesus taught his disciples to use; used in most Christian acts of worship

M

Mahabharata the longest poem in the world; written about second century BCE; contains nearly 100 000 verses; one of the two epics of the Hindus

Makkah birthplace of the prophet Muhammad and

Truth, spirituality and contemporary issues

Glossary continued ...

the spiritual heart of Islam; situated in Saudi Arabia

Mandir a Hindu place of worship

Mantra a sacred formula or chant; used in Hindu, Sikh and Buddhist worship

Martyr person who loses their life or suffers greatly because of their religious beliefs

Materialism a lifestyle that recognises the importance of the material element in life, but not the spiritual

Meditation spiritual discipline used in several religions; quietening the soul by concentrating the mind on a mantra or an object

Meeting houses name of Quaker place of worship

Mercy killing term used for euthanasia

Methodist Church a protestant Christian denomination which came into being through the preaching of Anglican priest John Wesley (1703–91)

Mezuzah biblical texts inscribed on a parchment in a small container fastened to the door-posts of Jewish homes

Minaret tower, usually part of a mosque, from which the muezzin calls the Muslim faithful to prayer five times a day

Miscarriage the spontaneous abortion of an embryo or foetus; usually at an early stage in a pregnancy

Moksha liberation from the cycle of birth, death and rebirth in Hinduism; achieved by knowledge, work or devotion

Monastery house of a male religious community

Monk member of male religious community; Christian Monks live under vows of poverty, chastity and obedience

Mool mantra the Sikh statement of belief; taken from the early chapters of the Guru Granth Sahib

Mosque Muslim building for public worship

Muhammad prophet of Allah; received visions from Allah which, as the Qur'an, became the basis of Islam; he organised a body of followers who became the first Muslims

Mukti another term for moksha, meaning 'release'

Murti a Hindu image of god

N

Nam Sanskrit word meaning 'name'; used in Sikhism as the name for God

New Testament the second part of the Christian Bible, contains the Christian scriptures including the four Gospels and the Epistles

Nuclear family a couple and their children

Nun member of a religious order of women; Christian nuns live under vows of poverty, chastity and obedience

O

Old Testament title used in the Christian church for Jewish Scriptures; the first part of the Christian Bible

Orthodox Church originally the church of the eastern region of the Roman Empire; separation of the eastern (Orthodox) and western (Catholic) regions came about in 1054CE

P

Palliative care care for the terminally ill and their families

Passive euthanasia withholding treatment from incurable patients until they die

Passover important Jewish festival held each year; commemorates the exodus of the Jews from Egyptian slavery with God's help

Paul (St) originally a persecutor of early Christians; converted after a vision of Christ; became a tireless missionary; many books by Paul included in the New Testament

Penance penalty imposed in Roman Catholic Church on those who are seeking the forgiveness of their sins

Pope leader of the world's Roman Catholics; believed to be the successor of St Peter, the most prominent of the disciples of Jesus

Poverty trap when someone on benefits gets a poorly-paid job and they lose their benefit, so leaving them worse off than before

Prayer words, spoken or thought, to God in worship

Priest title given to people in Christianity and Hinduism who officiate in public worship and other religious ceremonies

Protestant members of the Christian Church other than Roman Catholic or Orthodox; they reject the authority of the Pope and follow the text of the Bible

Puja term used in Hinduism and Buddhism for the worship or reverence paid to the gods or superior beings

Purim Jewish festival celebrating success of Queen Esther in saving many Jews from massacre planned by Haman, their enemy

Q

Quakers Christian society which began in the seventeenth century; largely silent form of worship; opposed to war

Qur'an the sacred book of Islam

R

Rabbi (my master), title given to authorised teacher in a Jewish community and leader of worship

Ramadan ninth month of Muslim year; observed as month of fasting, one of the five pillars of Islam

Recreational drugs drugs which are taken for non-medical use; part of the recreational life of person

Reht Maryada code of conduct in Sikhism

Reincarnation belief held by Hindus, Sikhs and Buddhists that each person goes through many rebirths

Relative poverty poverty which is relative to the lifestyle enjoyed by other people in the same society

Resurrection the raising of the dead

Roman Catholic Church community of Christians throughout the world, which offers allegiance to the Pope as the successor of St Peter

Rosary string of beads used to help people when praying, often enabling them to keep count during their devotion

S

Sabbath special day of rest observed by Jews and Christians; following example of God who rested after six days spent creating the world

Sacrament a special Christian service, such as Holy Communion, which is believed to convey a divine blessing to those who take part

Sadhu a Hindu holy man

Salah the second pillar of Islam - praying five times a day

Salvation Army Protestant organisation formed by William and Catherine Booth in 1865; conducts open-air services and forms of social work; has a distinctive uniform

Samaritans (The) organisation based in the UK, set up to provide counselling to people in distress and considering suicide

Sanskrit ancient language of India used to write the Hindu scriptures and epic poems

Sawm the fourth pillar of Islam – fasting during Ramadan

Sermon on the Mount a collection of the teachings of Jesus found in Matthew 5–7

Shabbat (Sabbath) Jewish day of rest

Shahadah the first pillar of Islam – the basic belief of Islam in Allah and his prophet, Muhammad

Shariah laws which are based solely on the teaching of the Qur'an

Siddartha Gotama founder of Bhuddism

Spirituality a recognition that human beings have a spiritual, as well as a material, dimension

Sudra the Hindu worker caste

Suicide the taking of one's own life, intentionally, without assistance from someone else

Surrogacy woman having a baby for someone else

Suttee the practice, now illegal, of Hindu widows throwing themselves on the funeral pyre of their husband

Symbol an item that represents something

Synagogue 'gathering together'; a place of learning and instruction for Jews

Truth, spirituality and contemporary issues

Glossary continued ...

T

Tagging fitting an electronic device to someone released from prison so the authorities know where they are and what they are doing

Tallit Jewish prayer shawl of mainly white material with fringes; worn by males at morning prayer and all services on Day of Atonement

Talmud major source of Jewish law

Tanakh Jewish term for scriptures; derived from initials for three sections of the book – Torah, Neviim and Kethuvim,

Teetotalism completely abstaining from drinking alcohol

Tefillin two small leather boxes, containing passages of scripture, attached to arm and forehead by Jewish men during prayer; also called 'phylacteries'

Ten Commandments in the Bible, the rules of conduct given by God to Moses on Mount Sinai and written on tablets of stone; they also form part of the 613 commandments in the Torah

Therapeutic cloning cloning parts of the body, which can then be used to cure specific diseases and illnesses

Tithe custom of giving one-tenth of an individual's income or produce to God; carried on by Jews and Christians who give proportion of their income to needy causes

Torah (law), the first five books of the Jewish scriptures – Genesis, Exodus, Deuteronomy, Leviticus and Numbers; most important part of the Jewish scriptures

Trinity in Christianity the three persons of God – God the Father, God the Son and God the Holy Spirit

Tzedakah Jewish charitable giving

U

Ummah Muslims bound together by religious ties

V

Vaisya trader/farmer in Hindu caste system

Varna Hindu idea, based on caste, of position in society

Vedas Hindu holy Scriptures

Vicar man or woman in charge of Church of England church

Vocation (calling), term used in Christianity to those 'called' to religious life as a priest, monk or nun

W

Watershed the voluntary code of conduct preventing films that portray sexual and violent themes being shown before 9pm on UK terrestrial television

Welfare state situation in the UK where medical and educational facilities are all provided by the state, especially to those in financial need

Wudu washing ritual performed by Muslims before praying

Y

Yoga spiritual discipline involving meditation and adoption of certain body positions

Yom Kippur Hebrew name for Day of Atonement

Z

Zakat third pillar of Islam – requirement that all Muslims give part of their income to help the needy

Truth, spirituality and contemporary issues

Useful contacts

General addresses

The Buddhist Society
58 Eccleston Square
London SW1V 1PH
020 7834 5858
www.thebuddhistsociety.org.uk.

Catholic Truth Society
40–6 Harleyford Road
London SE11 5AY
020 7640 0042
www.cts-online.org.uk/

The Children's Society
Edward Rudolf House
Margery Street
London WC1X 0JL
020 7841 4400
www.the-childrens-society.org.uk

Church of England Information Office
Church House
Great Smith Street
London SW1P 3NZ
020 7898 1000
www.cofe.anglican.org

Dharmapala Building
The Dharmapala
The Avenue
Chiswick
London W4 1UD
020 8995 9493
www.londonbuddhistvihara.co.uk

The Islamic Foundation
Markfield Conference Centre
Ratby Lane
Markfield
Leicestershire LE67 9SY
01530 244 944
www.islamic-foundation.org.uk

Jewish Care
221 Golders Green Road
London NW11 9DQ
020 8922 2000
www.jewishcare.org/

London Buddhist Centre
51 Roman Road
Bethnal Green
London E2 OHU
0845 458 4716
www.lbc.org.uk

Ramakrishna Vedanta Centre
Blind Lane
Bourne End
Buckinghamshire SL8 5LG
01628 526 464
www.vedantauk.com

Religious Society of Friends (Quakers)
Friends House
173 Euston Road
London NW1 2BJ
020 7663 1135
www.quaker.org.uk

Salvation Army
PO Box 249
101 Newington Causeway
London SE1 6BN
0845 634 0101
www.salvationarmy.org.uk

Matters of life and death

LIFE Organisation
Life House
Newbold Terrace
Leamington Spa
Warwickshire CV32 4EA
01926 421 587
www.lifeuk.org

St Christopher's Hospice
51–59 Lawrie Park Road
Sydenham
London SE26 6DZ
0208 778 9252
0870 903 3 903
www.hospiceinformation.info

Samaritans
Upper Mill
Kingston Road
Ewell
Surrey KT17 2AF
020 8394 8344
08457 90 90 90
www.samaritans.org

Voluntary Euthanasia Society
13 Prince of Wales Terrace
London W8 5PG
020 7937 7770
www.ves.org.uk

Drugs

DrugScope
32–36 Loman Street
London SE1 0EE
020 7928 1211
www.drugscope.org.uk

Truth, spirituality and contemporary issues

Useful contacts continued ...

Media

BBC Religious Broadcasting
New Broadcasting House
Oxford Road
Manchester M60 1SJ
0161 200 2020
www.bbc.co.uk

Channel 4 TV
124 Horseferry Road
London SW1P 2TX
020 7396 4444
www.channel4.com

Crime and punishment

Amnesty International
99–119 Rosebery Avenue
London ECIR 4RE
020 7814 6200
www.amnesty.org

The Muslim College
20–22 Creffield Road
Ealing Common
London W5 3RP
020 8992 6636
www.muslimcollege.ac.uk

Prison Advice & Care Trust
Lincoln House
1–3 Brixton Road
London SW9 6DE
020 7582 1313
www.imprisonment.org.uk

Rich and poor

Catholic Agency for Overseas Development (CAFOD)
2 Romero Close
Stockwell Road
London SW9 9TY
020 7733 7900
www.cafod.org.uk

Christian Aid
35 Lower Marsh
London SE1 7RT
020 7620 4444
www.christian-aid.org.uk

Gingerbread
7 Sovereign Close
Sovereign Court
London EIW 3HW
020 7488 9300
www.gingerbread.org.uk

Help the Aged
207–21 Pentonville Road
London N1 9UZ
020 7278 1114
www.helptheaged.org.uk

Islamic Relief
19 Rea Street South
Birmingham B5 6LB
0121 605 5555
www.islamic-relief.com/uk

Muslim Aid
PO Box 3
London NW1 7UB
020 7387 7171
www.muslimaid.org

Oxfam
Oxfam House
274 Banbury Road
Oxford OX2 7DZ
01865 312 610
www.oxfam.org.uk

Save the Children Fund
17 Grove Lane
London SE5 8RD
020 7703 5400
www.savethechildren.org.uk

Shelter
88 Old Street
London EC1V 9HU
020 7505 4699
www.shelter.org.uk

The Swaminarayan Hindu Mission
105–119 Brentfield Road
Neasden
London NW10 8JP
020 8965 2651
www.swaminarayan.org

Tear Fund
100 Church Road
Teddington
Middlesex TW11 8QE
020 8977 9144
www.tearfund.org

World Jewish Relief
The Forum
74–80 Camden Street
London NW1 0EG
020 7691 1775
www.wjr.org.uk

Truth, spirituality and contemporary issues

Index

Absolute poverty 119, 122, 123
Ahimsa 64, 65
AID 34, 44, 46
AIH 34, 44, 46
Akhand Path 8
Alcohol 67, 68, 70, 71, 78, 80, 82, 116
Allah 6, 16, 24, 40, 44, 62, 63, 80, 97, 115, 132
Altar 16
Amrit 10, 116
Ashram 12
AUM 17
Bible 2, 8, 9, 22
Blasphemy 85, 94, 97
Blood transfusions 40, 42
Brahman 6, 17, 26
Brahmin 116, 117
Buddha 2, 10, 26
Capital punishment 104, 108, 110, 114, 115
Caste 116, 117
Cathedral 14, 20
Church of England 43, 113, 124
Class A drugs 67, 74, 75
Class B drugs 67, 76, 77
Cloning 29, 36, 37, 38, 39, 42, 44, 46
Crime 102, 103
Cross 16, 17
Day of Atonement 114, 115
Drugs 67, 68, 72, 77, 78, 80, 82
Easter 11, 18
Elderly 50, 51, 60, 62, 64

Embryology 44, 46
Euthanasia 32, 33, 54, 55, 60, 61, 62, 64
Faith communities 1, 2, 12, 14
Fasting 16, 24, 25
Five Pillars of Islam 16, 24, 25, 132, 133
Five Precepts 64, 82, 99
Gambling 119, 128, 130, 132
Genetic Engineering 29, 36, 37, 42, 44, 46
Gospels 8, 9, 20, 22
Gurdwara 82, 116
Guru 12, 13, 26
Guru Granth Sahib 3, 26
Guru Nanak 26, 82
Hajj 16, 24, 25
Holy books 9, 10, 20, 29, 98, 116, 132
Holy Communion 11, 16, 17, 18, 22
Holy Spirit 22, 23
Hospice Movement 52, 53, 54
Icon 20, 22, 23
Illegal drugs 67, 78
Imam 10, 11
Infertility 34, 35, 42, 43, 44, 46
Internet 85, 86, 90, 98
In vitro fertilisation 34, 42, 44, 46
Jehovah's Witnesses 40, 41
Jesus 12, 16, 17, 20, 22, 60, 78, 85, 112, 113, 130, 131
Jihad 8, 62
Karma 64, 65, 134
Khalsa 10, 17, 26

Truth, spirituality and contemporary issues

Index continued ...

Legal drugs 69, 70
Lotto 119, 120, 128
Makkah 16, 17, 24
Mantra 18, 19, 26
Materialism 4, 5
Media 85, 86, 88, 90, 94, 96, 98
Meditation 15, 18
Mezuzah 16, 17
Minaret 16, 17
Monk 10, 12, 13, 18, 26
Mosque 16, 17
Muhammad 2, 14, 24, 63, 80, 97, 115
Nam 6, 26
New Testament 8, 9, 13
Nun 10, 12, 13, 18, 26
Old Testament 8, 9
Orthodox Church 10, 22
Passover 10, 11
Paul 8
Pope 10, 22
Poverty 122, 124, 132, 134
Poverty trap 120, 122, 123, 126
Priest 10, 12
Punishment 101, 104, 106, 112, 114, 116
Quakers 14, 15, 22
Qur'an 2, 3, 6, 9, 24, 44, 80, 97, 108, 114
Rabbi 10, 11, 44
Ramadan 16, 17, 24
Reincarnation 30, 64, 116
Relative poverty 119, 122, 123

Reht Maryada 116, 117
Roman Catholic Church 9, 10, 18, 19, 22, 34, 42, 43, 60, 94
Rosary 14, 22
Sabbath day 24, 32, 96
Sadhu 26, 82
Salvation Army 12, 13, 22
Shahadah 16, 24, 25
Shariah 62, 63, 97, 108, 114, 115
Single parents 122, 124
Smoking 67, 68, 71, 78, 80, 82
Suicide 32, 58, 59, 60, 62, 63, 64
Surrogacy 34, 35, 44, 46
Symbols 16, 17
Talmud 24, 80, 96
Tanakh 24, 25, 44
Television 86, 88, 90, 92, 94
Ten Commandments 2, 3, 24, 60
Therapeutic Cloning 38, 39, 43
Torah 2, 3, 9, 24, 44, 62
Trinity 22, 23
Voluntary Euthanasia Society (EXIT) 54, 56
Voluntary Organisations 12, 126
Watershed 88, 90, 91
Wealth 130, 132, 134
Welfare state 51, 122
Worship 2, 10, 12, 14, 15, 22, 92
Wudu 18, 80